the art of
empowerment

Charlyne '99.

啓
発

the art of
empowerment

the profit and pain of
employee involvement

RON JOHNSON
DAVID REDMOND

FINANCIAL TIMES
PITMAN PUBLISHING

FINANCIAL TIMES

MANAGEMENT

LONDON · SAN FRANCISCO
KUALA LUMPUR · JOHANNESBURG

Financial Times Management delivers the knowledge,
skills and understanding that enable students,
managers and organisations to achieve their ambitions,
whatever their needs, wherever they are.

London Office:
128 Long Acre, London WC2E 9AN
Tel: +44 (0)171 447 2000
Fax: +44 (0)171 240 5771
Website: www.ftmanagement.com

A Division of Financial Times Professional Limited

First published in Great Britain in 1998

ISBN 0 273 63093 8

British Library Cataloguing in Publication Data
A CIP catalogue record for this book can be obtained from the British Library.

10 9 8 7 6 5 4 3 2

Typeset by Northern Phototypesetting Co Ltd, Bolton
Printed and bound in Great Britain by Biddles Ltd, Guildford and Kings Lynn

The Publishers' policy is to use paper manufactured from sustainable forests.

About the authors

Ron Johnson, an independent consultant since 1980, specializes in corporate strategy and the management of change. He has been Direc-tor of Training at the Manpower Services Commission and twice Vice President (T&D) of the Institute of Personnel Man-agement. Over recent years, his main clients have been a selection of well-known PLCs including BICC, Cadbury and British Airways. He spends his time helping people to plan and to manage organizational development, focusing on the business, the operation and the people issues. He is equally  at home working with the directors of large corporations, senior pub-lic officials, trade unionists, sole traders and shop floor workers. Ron has taken a particular interest in assisting organizations to introduce teamworking throughout entire operational units. He is an experi-enced public speaker and the author of a number of books on manag-ing people, teamwork and business planning.

David Redmond's extensive career in human resource management in the UK and overseas culminated in his appointment as Director of Human Resources in BOC Distribution Services, a major international distribution company serving Marks & Spencer, Sainsbury, Safeway and Tesco. During his 20 years with BOC Distribution Services, David pioneered many developments in employee communications and participation. He took  part in a number of employee involvement initiatives with the Institute of Personnel & Development and the Involve-ment & Participation Association. David worked closely with trade unions in developing these initiatives. Since 1990, David has con-ducted a number of consultancy assignments concerned with employee relations, training, management development and quality programmes.

**'We cannot be a beacon to the world
unless the talents of all the people
shine through.'**

TONY BLAIR
Prime Minister, United Kingdom

From his speech at the Labour Party Conference,
30 September 1997

Contents

List of figures and tables   x

Foreword by Meredith Belbin   xi

A note from John Monks, General Secretary of the Trades Union Congress   xiii

Acknowledgements   xiv

Introduction   xv

Part I · The essentials of empowerment

1 What is empowerment?   *3*
All your essential questions answered

Achieving organizational goals · Empowerment values · Extent of employee involvement · Workers' representatives · *Progress checklist*

2 Benefits and pitfalls   *17*
Achieving gains for the organization and avoiding costly mistakes

Tangible benefits · Potential pitfalls · Power and authority · Expectations · Building trust · *Progress checklist*

3 Managing the culture change   *31*
A step-by-step guide to the mechanics of making the change

Strategic objectives · Management commitment · Review of systems · Information management and staff development · Project management · *Ten action points · Progress checklist*

4 Rewards and empowerment   *45*
Aligning your reward systems to support the empowerment culture

Culture and rewards · Winners and losers · Non-financial rewards · *Progress checklist*

5 Choosing the approach   *57*
Finding the best way for your particular organization to succeed

Quality and customer care · Organizational renewal · Learning and development · Communications · Teamwork · Selecting the method · *Progress checklist*

Part II · Involvement methods

6 Initiating change 73
More detail on methods to get you started

Strategic change · Data and discussion · Management workshops · Conducting a survey · Coaching and counselling · *Progress checklist*

7 Working relationships 91
How to get the roles and structures right

Empowered work groups · Empowered structures: Consultation and negotiation · New roles for old · *Progress checklist*

8 Informing people 99
Effective methods for disseminating information

Regular written information · Regular face-to-face briefings · Representational groups · Special events · Person-to-person responsibilities · Work groups and project groups · Multidirectional flows · *Progress checklist*

9 Generating feedback 113
How to generate and handle feedback

Large meetings · Teamwork workshops · Team briefings · Focus groups and brainstorming sessions · Surveys and suggestion schemes · Dynamic interaction · *Progress checklist*

10 Sharing and negotiating 125
How and when to share decisions

Delegation · Delegation of communications · Joint decisions Negotiation and effort bargains · Formal structures · *Progress checklist*

11 Managing business relationships 139
Managing the interfaces with stakeholders

Shareholders' concerns · Customer focus · Employees and 'portfolio people' · Suppliers and in-house contractors · Community concerns · *Progress checklist*

Part III · Learning and empowerment

12 Learning and development 151
An overview of ways of helping people to learn

Learning by means of formal training and education · Learning at work · Coaching, counselling and mentoring · Appraisals · *Progress checklist*

13 Planned learning *163*
Planning learning to achieve organizational goals

Strategic planning · Open learning · Management development · Training for the task · Monitoring and evaluating results · *Progress checklist*

14 Empowering individuals *173*
Ways and means to help your people to grow

Job concepts · Developing ability · Equal opportunities · Authority and opportunity · *Progress checklists*

15 Organizational learning and teamwork *185*
Creating a dynamic learning organization

The holistic view · Organization-wide teamwork · Team processes · Sharing visions and goals · Sharing an understanding of how things work · Valued and aspiring individuals · *Progress checklist*

16 Leading an empowered organization *195*
Developing the leadership you need to succeed

Management style · Leadership qualities · Learning to lead · *Progress checklist*

Part IV · Next steps

17 Facing the future *205*
Now you must consider what action you will take

Employment patterns · Retaining talent · Core values · Management style · Trade unions · World trade · Employee commitment · Conclusion · *Progress checklist*

Appendix – A beginner's guide to empowerment: how to get started *211*

Further reading *215*

Index *221*

List of figures and tables

Figure 1   The essential steps to empowerment   *10*
Figure 2   Levels of delegation   *37*
Figure 3   A committee structure that helps effective communications   *126*
Figure 4   The teamwork formula   *190*

Table 1   Is yours an empowered or command and control culture?   *48*
Table 2   Empowerment matrix   *95*

Note: the Japanese symbol used on the cover and on various pages of this book means 'empowerment'.

Foreword

by Meredith Belbin

According to Ron Johnson and David Redmond, empowerment is an art. I believe, emphatically, that they are right. Those who cling to certainties or who like the precision of what is termed 'scientific management' should be made aware that that empowerment offers no guaranteed benefits. If asked to generalise on how empowerment has fared in practice, on the basis of the studies of which I am aware, I must admit that they commonly show little positive gain, and have often been followed by a swing of the pendulum and a reversion to hierarchical management. In contrast, the limited number of times when it has been applied and has been successful, it has been spectacularly successful. The question arises as to why such a wide variation in outcomes should exist.

The answer, I believe, lies in the art of knowing where to begin, in understanding the culture of the workplace and in the timing of critical actions and decisions. In a way, this is a book about people and how they behave in particular situations; it presents lively Snapshots (windows on the world of those who have succeeded) and introduces the reader to valued practices rather than to any set formula of recommended procedures.

So, how should this book be read? You could start at the beginning and read through to the end. But, for most people, this is not something I would recommend as the range of material covered could blur in the mind if you try to remember it as a whole. Rather, this is a book to dip into, for there are pearls of wisdom that are quickly lost if the book is read at speed and without reflection.

My suggestion would be to look at the Contents page with a view to perusing any section that looks relevant to current problems. This could be a useful counter to the propensity of many managers to be drawn by habit and reflex to particular solutions without considering alternative approaches. The educated manager is better placed to 'read first, decide afterwards'. But, for all that there is a need to heed the saying 'It is better to make the right decision slowly than the wrong decision quickly'.

A complex area demands a strategic approach. In this connection, Figure 1 deserves special attention. Empowerment lies at the sophisticated end of the communication process. Informing is the first and most elementary stage since everyone does it. Those who talk most listen least. Consulting as a two-way process is therefore a step forward, for it requires communication balance – more difficult to achieve than people think. Sharing means accepting a measure of joint ground or ownership, a condition that calls for maturity of character and temperament. Delegating can only come about when there is well-founded trust in the ability of a designated individual or individuals to make decisions in a defined area. Empowerment, at the ultimate end of the chain, demands an extension of a trust that has been through a proving process to cover an even broader field of responsibility.

It is not easy for managers to stand back and look at the total picture when assigning work. Many good operational managers in due course, as their remits increase, encounter problems in distinguishing between tasks and responsibility, whether in words or action. Tasks relate to items of work given to a job holder by a person in authority; responsibility, in contrast, is attached solely to an outcome, for which the job holder is made accountable, irrespective of how the work is tackled. The temptation to assign responsibility and then to interfere in the execution of the work is something many managers find irresistible.

The lesson, for me, is that, in the evolution towards empowerment, we must learn to master one stage before we can tackle the next. Great maturity is needed before a manager is fitted to empower others and with results that confirm the soundness of the theory that underlines the approach. And here I must declare my belief in the essential unity of theory and practice. That position has also been the mark of Ron Johnson, who has, further, always applied his beliefs with the courage of his convictions and with commendable results, as I can testify over the long years of our close association. I am glad, too, that David Redmond has been able to bring to bear his academic studies of this area and his extensive experience as Human Resources Director. Together they have produced a book that I believe will run for many years as the definitive work on this important subject.

Meredith Belbin

A note

from the General Secretary of the Trades Union Congress

Trade unions are built on the principles of empowerment – empowering their members to achieve more together than they could hope to achieve as isolated individuals. Genuine empowerment at the workplace will therefore be understood and welcomed by union members. But union members will also be cautious of managers bearing new concepts – too often ideas like flexibility have bent all one way.

To help us meet the challenges of rapid change in the world of work, we need to understand and implement fairly and effectively concepts like empowerment. That is why this book will be welcomed by trade unionists and forward-looking managers alike.

John Monks
General Secretary of the TUC

Acknowledgements

We thank Dr Meredith Belbin (Belbin Associates) and Professor John Fyfe (W. S. Atkins) for helpful discussions. We are grateful to all the companies and public-sector bodies that have allowed us to work with them in empowering people. We also record our appreciation of the people and organizations that have helped us with information and advice, especially in connection with the preparation of Snapshots, notably Miss J. P. Young, Personnel Manager, BICC Blackley; Peter Brinsden, Managing Director, BOC Distribution Services; David Moss, Managing Director, Valvestock; Laurence Murrell, Managing Director, Torquay Leisure Hotels; Jane Bevan, Public Relations Manager, The Natural History Museum; Stella Jackson, Head of Management Development, Lewisham Borough Council; Mr P. K. Waring, Personnel Manager, Operations, Cadbury Limited; and Michael Davey, Regional Secretary, TGWU.

Finally, we share John Monks' concern that empowerment concepts need to be implemented fairly and effectively, and we are grateful to him for allowing us to include a note on his views in this book.

Introduction

Empowerment is about achieving organizational goals; it means getting every-one involved in making a success of the business. Involving people is no longer an option, it is a requirement for success. The move towards empower-ment can bring great gains, but it can also be a disappointment if it is misman-aged. It is certainly not an easy option. This book does not tell you how to run your business, but if you seriously want to set about involving all your people in a joint endeavour to make your organization successful, read on.

The bottom line is that organizations seek to empower people to achieve pos-itive improvements in performance. Senior executives have come to realize that the people within organizations represent a crucial resource, a force that can be harnessed for the good of the enterprise.

Empowerment is also about values. It is about treating people in a different way. It involves seeing people as whole human beings with their own hopes and fears, their own aspirations and their own lives outside the workplace. Empow-ered people are treated with respect. Their views are heeded. Their talents are used. They are treated fairly, praised for work well done and criticized construc-tively. They are prepared to work wholeheartedly with others in a worthwhile enterprise.

Empowerment is not black and white. We have not actually found any of these mythical totally 'empowered organizations', but we have decided to speak as if they exist because the concept presents a goal towards which management can strive. We have found many organizations that are on the road to empowerment and where, in part, it has been achieved. The question is, how far are you, as a director, prepared to go? As Meredith Belbin suggests in his Foreword, you can read the book right through or you can scan the Contents pages and go to the sec-tions that interest you.

We conceive of teamwork as an organization-wide activity with the focus being on developing team workers rather than developing teams as such. In our view, teams form spontaneously when a group of people trained in teamwork come to share a common goal and are prepared to work together to achieve it.

The Snapshots presented are mostly based on actual events that we have per-sonally been associated with in one way or another over the past decade. A few are derived from published information followed up by contact with the people concerned. They illustrate specific aspects of the matter under discussion, but do not purport to be examples of 'fully empowered' organizations. Most of the organizations we have dealt with have moved towards empowerment and the Snapshots often show one or more of the steps involved.

We have used the masculine and the feminine gender indiscriminately, except where we are writing about specific individuals.

We have worked closely with trade unions over many years. Many of our readers will be in organizations that recognize responsible trade unions. The book provides advice and guidance on how management in these organizations can work closely with trade unions in empowering the workforce.

We are conscious of the fact that people can use the same words but mean different things. Where we use a word that might be misunderstood, we have explained what we mean by the word and indicated this in bold type in the index.

PART I

The essentials of empowerment

啓
発

What is empowerment?

All your essential questions answered

- Empowerment is about achieving organizational goals: it means getting everyone involved in making a success of the business.

- Cultural values are an integral part of empowerment.

- Top management can involve employees at many levels and in many ways.

- Working with formal representatives can form part of the strategy.

- Developing empowerment requires painstaking care and patience.

Snapshot *The manager of a small BICC manufacturing unit in a keenly competitive market recognized the need for several changes. Increased productivity together with reduced scrap levels and throughput time had to be achieved. The amount of work in progress had to be cut down dramatically. Delays in achieving delivery dates to customers had to be tackled aggressively, and quality enhanced.*

The managers concluded that they needed a workforce that was more flexible, more conscious of priorities, more dedicated to quality assurance and more careful in the use of materials. They decided to introduce teamwork, starting with the management team. At the same time the unit was reorganized into product cells rather than the former process lines.

This gave the operatives a greater sense of pride in the cables produced. They were given responsibility for the quality of the products. They were encouraged to work with management on the improvement of the operation. They were given training in Just in Time (JIT) methods. Over a period of months the management style changed, the workforce responded and a new working culture emerged.

Work in progress was reduced dramatically. Quality improved, scrap was reduced and the efficiency of the plant in meeting production targets exceeded expectations. Absenteeism reduced. The empowered workforce delivered material benefits to the unit. The operatives also reported that it was a better, happier place to work.

Achieving organizational goals

Empowerment is not a soft option. Directors and senior managers who set off down the road towards employee empowerment do so because they believe there are definable organizational goals that cannot be met without involving the entire workforce. The organization needs all their knowledge, experience and skills – as well as their energetic commitment to the company aims and objectives. Empowerment is generally seen as part of an overall plan to achieve organizational improvements in areas such as operational effectiveness, quality management, customer care and continuous improvement.

An empowered organization needs clear goals and firm leadership. The process starts when directors and senior managers spend time setting organizational goals. They need to think through the contribution of empowerment (and concomitant initiatives) to these goals, and to commit themselves to the programme of change, including the personal costs involved. These personal costs include giving attention to empowerment values (see below) and spending time working with others to demonstrate and to promote new behaviours.

A vital component of success in any organization is the quality of the decisions its people make. Information is power. Only people who have relevant information can make sensible decisions. In the past, many decisions have been made by people at the top because they alone had the relevant information and the ability to interpret this information. As organizations grow, this becomes less practical. In larger organizations, as information has been processed upwards it has become distorted by aggregation and simplification.

'As information is passed upwards, it becomes distorted by aggregation and simplification.'

It has long been known that the most effective decisions are made by people as near as possible to the point where information is generated. Often this means people on the shop floor – in the laboratory, at the computer terminal, at the sales counter or operating the production machinery. Now, through new technology, these people can have the information. If they have the ability to interpret this, they can make many of the decisions formerly made by managers. This will work well provided that the people concerned are wholeheartedly committed to the organization's goals.

An organization is empowered when people have the information they need to make decisions about the operation in which they are engaged, the motivation to make these decisions in the best interests of the organization and the authority to make these decisions (these three key issues – authority to make decisions, having available information and appropriate motivation – are considered in more detail in Chapter 3). The limits of authority will change over time in a dynamic way as people gain more knowledge and experience, and as management gains more confidence in the operatives' ability to make sound decisions.

Snapshot *The organization had 100 advisers covering England, Scotland and Wales. They each worked from home, but were divided into 12 groups, each led by a manager. They needed clerical support from the centre, but they found that each time they telephoned, they spoke to a different clerk. Messages were mislaid, urgent requests became lost in the system. The field advisers became increasingly frustrated.*

The director decided to divide the work of the clerical support staff so that when an adviser telephoned head office support, she would be answered by one of two individuals. These individuals were given greater authority to make decisions and to follow through the requests they initiated than had been the case in the past. This meant that the support staff at head office started to take a personal interest in the advisers they helped and made a point of ensuring that their needs were met.

Information was now passed on without fail and urgent requests were followed up with diligence. Both the support staff and the field advisers felt they had more information and personal control over their work. Both groups expressed satisfaction with the new system.

An organization is empowered when everyone is involved in making a success of the business. There are, of course, degrees of empowerment, and it is possible to find organizations where there is involvement and empowerment in some sections but not in others.

Empowerment is not black and white: there are not fully empowered organizations and totally unempowered organizations. In most organizations there is already a degree of empowerment. The question is, how far are you, as a director, prepared to go?

Empowerment values

When directors and senior managers start to think seriously about empowerment, they must recognize that it requires commitment to a particular set of values. Empowerment is based on the notion that if you create the right conditions you can trust people to do their best for the organization. This means that people are valued, their opinions sought and their views taken into account. It means trusting people. You cannot expect to trust people if they cannot trust you. Empowerment requires a high level of honesty, openness and integrity on the part of top management. In many organizations, this level of mutual trust does not exist. It has to be built up and 'earned' over a period of time if empowerment is to be achieved.

> *'Empowerment means trusting people and you cannot expect to trust people if they cannot trust you.'*

This value system is more than a set of aspirations. It develops into a culture and a way of life. The way people behave towards each other, starting at the top, must be consistent with these values. The values will be reflected in the reward system and the communications on a day-to-day basis. Adherence to these values is of far greater significance than the tools and techniques used.

Snapshot *The Board of a major insurance company recognized that there was a need to become more focused in its marketing strategy. Competition was becoming more intense. New regulations were introduced that required companies to disclose commission. Together, these pressures provoked a review of both the product range and the methods of presentation and sales. New savings and pension products had to be introduced to fend off competition. This involved transforming the processes and procedures for developing, selling and administering these products.*

The quality of the IT support, the marketing materials and the training of the people involved both in house and on the road was considered crucial. The Board decided to involve people at all levels in changing the company culture and developing a teamwork approach to its activities.

Over a period of several months, tough, measurable targets were set for groups of people, and achieved. The company was able to launch a new range of products successfully and to position itself to meet future challenges.

It is not easy to initiate and sustain consistent honesty, openness and trust. There is a particular problem with openness. As information is power, giving people more information means sharing power. There are some areas of information within the business – and in public-sector bodies, too – that are sensitive. Some information – even about decisions that have not yet been taken – can have an effect on share price, give the competitors an edge or cause concern to employees, suppliers or customers. In public bodies there are often discussions about policy decisions and if half-baked information about these discussions is leaked, it can cause unnecessary – sometimes distressing – repercussions.

Such reasons are often quoted as an excuse for keeping the workforce in the dark. So much so, that managers generally tend to ask what they can tell the workforce, but the real question should be, what can we *not* tell the workforce. The best way forward is for management to establish the habit of keeping the workforce informed as much as possible. Management must make it clear that there will be occasions when it is necessary to keep back information because of the reasons cited above.

Another 'value' issue is blame. When things go wrong in a 'command and control' structured organization, a common reaction is for management to seek to pin the blame on somebody. In an empowered organization, when things go wrong everybody – and we mean everybody – works together to find out what went wrong, to seek to take corrective action and to prevent a recurrence. If, after a thorough investigation, it is shown that someone behaved unwisely, then action is taken to help that person learn how to behave better in future. If someone behaved in a clearly irresponsible manner, then it may be that a measure of blame needs to be assigned or even disciplinary action taken. You will notice that blame is the very last thing to be considered. This is sometimes called a 'no blame' culture, although, as you will observe, there is room for blame in extreme cases.

It should by now be clear that empowerment is much more than setting up a series of formal meetings or committees. It means that managers:

● provide a considerable amount of information to the workforce

● respond positively to what workers have to say and contribute

● delegate many decisions to individuals and work groups.

Two-way trust has to be developed for such a situation to work effectively for the benefit of the company. In essence, for this level of delegation to succeed:

● the workers need a lot of information

● they need to understand the data so that they can make rational decisions

● they must be committed to the goals of the organization.

This commitment is vital if the decisions are to be in the best interests of the organization. These developments require high-quality management and fewer, better trained people.

In some cases, it is useful for the top management team to work out a 'management code' to set out the way managers and directors intend to behave towards each other, and towards other members of the workforce.

Extent of employee involvement

In many ways, empowerment is the pinnacle of employee involvement. Organizations can involve workers in decision making:

- as individuals
- in working groups
- by means of representational groups, for example, trade unions, staff associations or people directly elected to consultative councils or committees
- in a dynamic, organic way, that is, information flows freely as required and decisions are made by the people best able to make them, irrespective of their rank or title.

In each case there are various levels at which this involvement can take place. For example, it can involve:

- merely providing information
- discussions before some decisions are made
- an element of sharing in making decisions, which can vary from making joint decisions or delegating decision making to negotiating when making decisions.

This is illustrated in Figure 1. For simplicity, the levels of empowerment are illustrated as distinct steps, but individual topics will be tackled in different ways. In practice, in an empowered organization, activities at all five levels will be operating at the same time. These discrete steps may be taken at the individual, group or organization level. The best procedure is to take this process one step at a time – informing before consulting, consulting before sharing, sharing before delegating and finally moving to full empowerment.

'Empowerment is the pinnacle of employee involvement.'

The parties involved need to gain experience together with step one before proceeding to step two and so forth. At each stage, managers and workers will be testing each other in terms of honesty, openness and trustworthiness. Empowerment requires a high level of commitment and it is reached through this process of growing trust.

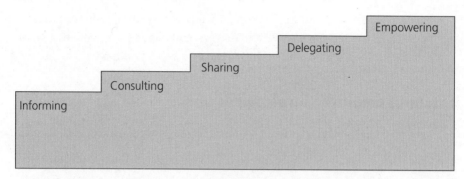

Figure 1 The essential steps to empowerment

The central activity in Figure 1 – sharing decisions – requires special attention. Joint decisions can be made where the interests of both 'sides' coincide. When the interests differ, this sharing inevitably takes the form of negotiation. This does not necessarily involve official negotiating machinery and the like – although this may be appropriate is some cases. Rather, generally, it means that there must be give and take so that both sides feel that they have benefited from the decision that has been made.

> **'Empowerment involves a high level of commitment.'**

When we speak of 'sides' here, we are not referring only to the possibility that a manager may want some of his people to do something they will find irksome, although this is one example of a practical situation where this may occur. It could well be that two managers have to negotiate the allocation of resources between their respective domains. In each case it is essential to distinguish between the common good and the personal or sectional interests concerned. This is one of the vital skills required to maintain effective empowerment.

> **Snapshot** *The Director of a division in the Civil Service was responsible for ten sections, each with a section head. He also had two deputy directors reporting to him. He decided that it was essential to keep in touch with the 12 managers in his division by means of a monthly meeting. There were three objectives he wanted to achieve through these meetings. He wanted to make sure his senior people were in touch with decisions made at higher levels in the department. He also wanted to have reports from his people so that he could keep his finger on the pulse of his division. The division faced a number of challenges and problems.* ▶

The Director wanted to provide an opportunity to discuss these matters with his senior managers and to take their views into account as new situations arose that required decisions to be made.

Very often, now each meeting consisted of three parts. The first part of the meeting was usually concerned with providing information, the director reporting back on decisions made at recent departmental meetings. There was no room here for discussion or consultation. The decisions had been made and that was that. He was, however, quite prepared to take questions and to seek to explain the reasons for decisions.

The second part of the meeting was, essentially, a 'business' meeting about the work of the division, each section reporting on progress and future plans. Discussion took place about future developments within the division and often decisions were made on key issues by two or three people at the meeting. When the Director was aware of decisions to be made at higher levels in the future, the meeting offered an opportunity to sound out the views of his senior people. The discussion was often directed at assessing the potential impact of these decisions on the division's work. Consultation and some sharing in decision making was taking place.

The third part of the meeting was often far more informal. People could open up to discussion any matter of concern, opportunities or problems. The Director often took a back seat. The managers had a real opportunity to influence events in their own sections and in the division as a whole. With persuasive arguments, these meetings could be the start of ideas that could influence the whole department.

In practical terms, management must be very clear about which topics are appropriate under each heading. It is patently dishonest, for example, to consult people about decisions that have already been made.

Snapshot   *In a large manufacturing unit it was customary for managers and technical people to design new equipment. All too often when the equipment was installed it was difficult to operate in practice. The equipment worked, but the operative needed extremely long arms or had to walk excessive distances between the control centre and the 'business end' of the machine.*

When the workforce became empowered, it became normal practice for the operatives to be involved in the project teams that designed new equipment and such stupidities were avoided.

Any management group that seeks to embark on increased involvement needs to think through:

- the mechanism of involvement (individual, group or representational)
- the tools to be used (for example, newsletters, briefing groups, consultative committees)
- the areas where discussions and sharing of decisions can be encouraged
- the extent to which people will be prepared to accept responsibility
- the system of rewards and the way this will influence people's behaviour.

By way of illustration, let us first consider the way an organization might deal with an individual employee.

- Management might simply provide *information* – about the job to be done, the methods to be used, the reward system, the training provided, key health and safety features.

  'It is dishonest to consult people about decisions that have already been made.'

- But management might be more forthcoming. A manager might *discuss* with the individual how the work is to be done, seeking her views on health and safety aspects of the task. They might talk over how the task fits into the scheme of things within the departments, and across other departments. There could be discussion about how the job should be rewarded, and how the job holder's skill and knowledge can be enhanced. Some of these topics are likely to be covered in discussions between senior people and their managers already.

- Management may consider that *decisions* on some of these topics might be then *shared*. An individual might be given the go ahead to use his or her dis-

cretion regarding how the job is done, the tools and methods to be used. He or she might be involved in discussions and have a share in the decisions made about new
equipment or changes in responsibilities. There is
already a body of literature on this subject at management level, but the principle can be applied at lower levels. The vast penetration of information systems means
that people on the shop floor have access to the information
they need to make crucial decisions about priorities and so forth.

'Improvement in technology gives people greater access to decision-making information.'

- Management may be content to leave some of the decision making to the employees themselves, given that they have the information and understanding required. This level of *delegation* assumes that the employees are willing to accept this level of responsibility and that they are committed to the organization's goals.

In taking this approach with a group, the subject expands.

- When providing *information* to work groups it is essential to specify goals in terms of outputs and methods, how work should be allocated and how the work of the group interfaces with other work groups.
- When it comes to engaging in *discussions* with work groups, these should not only focus on the question of what tasks are to be performed. There is an opportunity to discuss staffing levels, the allocations of responsibilities within the group, cooperation within the group, within the department, with other departments. The relevance of the tasks to the business as a whole and priorities for action can also be explored. The group can be consulted about the tools and equipment required to do the tasks, the raw materials provid-ed, the processes used and the information required. There can be discus-sions about how people in the group are rewarded. Topics may include what training and development they need and how this should be organized. The context within which the group operates, and even the appropriateness of the tasks to be performed, can be open to consideration. Managers may feel threatened by these processes.
- Many of the factors outlined above can become the subject of *sharing* in decision making. The work groups can often be left to manage work organi-zation, determine priorities and identify learning needs. Decisions about rewards must remain a matter for joint decision making (about how the rewards are shared) and negotiations must take place about how large the reward package is overall. Such delegation and sharing in decision making presumes that the employees concerned are committed to the organization's

goals, competent to make the decisions and provided with the information they need. Managers may feel unable to let go in some of these areas and they will need training, coaching and support.

Snapshot *An operational unit in a manufacturing company installed new computer-controlled machinery to make the product. Staff for the new plant were selected from existing employees on the basis of the skills needed to operate in this new environment. Management decided to 'empower' the workforce by training them:*

- *to undertake a range of tasks*
- *to act as team members both in work teams and in project teams to solve problems and to improve the operation – the managers themselves were trained in teamwork, team and project management.*

Because of teething troubles with the machinery, there were delays in training employees and this led to frustration. The machinery problems also meant that there was little time for people to meet and discuss operational issues.

As the mechanical problems were resolved, the training was completed and the people started to take a keen interest in the operation of the plant. Together, they took more responsibility, worked more effectively together and created a more congenial working environment. Regretfully, despite coaching and counselling, one manager was unable to adapt to the trusting and delegating style and had to be moved.

Increasing involvement implies that, at each stage, management is prepared to invest employees with more responsibility, and that the employees are prepared to accept this. Thus, the level of involvement should itself be a matter of ongoing discussion and agreement between management and the employees concerned.

Workers' representatives

There are various matters where it is appropriate for management to enter into discussions with representatives of the workforce. If the organization recognizes one or more trade unions, it is appropriate to use formal machinery to seek the cooperation and agreement of the workforce, particularly in such matters as reward schemes. The growth in works councils in various forms emphasizes the need for clear thinking on the part of management. The subjects for discussion with workers' representatives, whether in the context of meetings with trade union leaders or in works councils, must be carefully considered. Where will such discussions lead?

'Managers may feel unable to "let go" some decisions and need training, coaching and support.'

Such activity does not conflict with the drive towards empowerment, but it is a factor that must be borne in mind at the planning stage. Furthermore, management must not regard this as the only means of communication with the workforce. It must be seen as part of the overall strategy and as one of the mechanisms in the change management process.

Many of the factors that need to be taken into account and the importance of planning and managing change have been outlined in this chapter. The process of managing this change is covered in Chapter 3.

Progress checklist

Tick the following items when you can honestly answer 'Yes' to the question posed.

Are your organizational goals set out clearly? ❏

Have they been agreed at senior management levels? ❏

Has the top team thought through the full implications of empowerment and the implicit values? ❏

Have you decided to work towards openness and honesty in your organization? ❏

Are the most senior people prepared to build a bond of trust with the workforce? ❏

Have senior people thought through how they will behave towards each other and to subordinates in future? ❏

Have you decided to develop a culture where blame is the last matter to be considered when things go wrong? ❏

Have you and senior colleagues considered the extent to which you intend to involve and empower people, and the steps along the way to this end? ❏

Do you have a policy on how you will deal with employee representatives and trade union officers? ❏

If you have a works council, have you decided how its activities will relate to your empowerment initiatives? ❏

2

Benefits and pitfalls

Achieving gains for the organization and avoiding costly mistakes

- Enhancing business success by empowering the workforce.

- Achieving better decisions, flexibility, competence and continuous improvement.

- Planning to succeed and avoid the pitfalls.

- Coping with shifting power and authority.

- Dealing with expectations, job security and pay.

- Being careful if you decide to mount a survey.

- The uphill climb towards trust.

Snapshot *Valvestock is a company that sells and distributes industrial valves and actuators. It is part of Glynwed International PLC. Valvestock is characterized by a dedication to customer service. This customer concern stems mostly from the Managing Director himself, and permeates the organization.*

When you enter the front door, there is an immediate, warm and friendly greeting from the receptionist. When you sit waiting for a few moments to be ushered in to meet your contact, people who pass by will ask if you are OK or need anything. When you meet people in the offices and in the store rooms it is clear that there is a culture of helpfulness that pervades the place.

Listening to a conversation between a potential customer and the telephone salesperson, it became very clear that the aim of the salesperson was not to sell a product, but to make sure that the customer's needs were met. The company has found a user-friendly way to make use of its computer system. This enables the salesperson quickly to identify what products are in stock, and what the product can do. If there is any doubt at all in the salesperson's mind as to whether or not this product is right for the customer, he or she will be transferred then and there to a technical expert who will talk through the customer's problem and recommend a solution.

The mind-set of the staff is that making sure the customer has a solution to his or her problem is more important than making a sale. This same ethos of customer care extends to the warehouse and despatch areas where staff select items for delivery to customers, pack these items carefully and send them on their way.

Once they have been properly trained, people just get on and do what is necessary. Considerable attention is paid to the learning needs of people at all levels in the organization. Much of the training is given on the job, with judicious use of external training providers.

People in this organization have clear goals, information, ability through training and coaching, and authority to make decisions in the best interest of the business. It thrives.

Tangible benefits

The bottom line is that organizations seek to empower people because they believe that this improves the company performance in some way. Senior executives have come to realize that the people within organizations represent a crucial resource, a force that can be harnessed for the good of the enterprise.

Modern organizations require that better decisions be made, more quickly:

- to be more responsive to customer demand

- to be more reactive to competitor activity

- to be more efficient in the use of resources – materials, people, machinery, accommodation

- to be ready to take advantage of new technology and new methods

- to be more effective in delivering goods and services

- to maintain high levels of quality in all aspects of the operation

- to create a culture of continuous development.

These responses cannot be achieved simply by making better decisions at the top. Organizations need better, quicker decision making to take place at all levels. That is exactly what an empowered organization can achieve.

Snapshot *An organization specializing in IT had two different parts to its operation. One part specialized in providing in-depth consultancy, helping organizations to draw up specifications for computer systems. The other part provided an ongoing support service to similar organizations. Often staff from one part of the organization would pick up information that could provide leads for the other part, but these were infrequently passed on to those who could make use of them.*

Initially, the organization thought to solve this by setting up complicated communications systems to facilitate this exchange of information. They came to realize, however, that the need was not for better systems, but for:

- *better understanding between the people in the two arms of the organization*

- *more commitment to the organization as a whole.* ▶

Front-line staff needed to appreciate and understand the needs of their colleagues in other areas of work. They also needed to recognize that their futures were tied up with the success of the organization as a whole, not just with their own particular jobs and sections.

Organizations may start along this path from different points and tackle the problem in different ways depending, for example, on their primary operational concern. An organization that needs to improve its decision-making process may well embark on an education and training programme as a way into empowerment. An organization with a workforce resistant to change may embark on a teamwork training programme. A business where employees are insensitive to customer needs may start with a customer care programme. A company with quality problems may initiate a quality management programme. In every case, the ability and motivation of the workforce become key factors. If the change programme is properly managed, each could end up with an empowered organization.

'One of the benefits of empowerment is staff flexibility.'

One of the undoubted benefits of empowerment is staff flexibility. In an empowered organization anybody will do any job that needs to be done – provided he or she has the necessary skills. You will not hear people say 'that's not my job' when there is a need for some simple task to be done. As employees become more involved and are keen to achieve success on the job, they evince a desire to improve their knowledge and skills. They become more willing to share their skills with one another, to teach each other and learn from one another. The actual skill level of an empowered organization rises spontaneously so that jobs are carried out in a more competent fashion all along the line.

This desire for self and team improvement goes beyond the formal on-the-job learning. Management can respond by providing more formal training programmes, both on and off the job, as appropriate (see Part III for more details). Indeed, an empowered organization can evolve organically into a learning organization driven not by imposed appraisal and training systems but by a desire to improve performance (see Chapter 15 for more information about learning organizations).

There is a desire to improve the job, which is manifest in the way that people are willing to try out new ideas, seeking ways to make them work, instead of reasons for not trying. These ideas may be their own or they may come from other people. The 'not invented here' syndrome has no place in an empowered organization. Innovation and continuous improvement become a way of life, not unusual events.

We consider that good housekeeping is a useful indicator of organizational health. As you wander around the premises, are the gangways clear? Is rubbish tidied away? Are machine tools cleaned and stored carefully? Are desks tidy or piled high with odd bits of paper? Are the electrical wires of office equipment neatly stowed or flopping about in a dangerous fashion? Is stock tidily stacked away and properly labelled? Does everybody have a part to play in maintaining this state? In an empowered organization, people want to keep their working environment tidy and take a pride in their workplace. This orderliness is not just 'skin deep', it extends to the way equipment is maintained, tools are stored and materials handled.

> *'Innovation and continuous improvement become a way of life.'*

Snapshot *In a large warehouse we observed in the distance a consignment of goods on the move. An item fell off the trailer. The driver could not observe this from his position. Two other people passing by the trailer and the fallen item ignored the incident completely. They clearly considered that items in the gangway were not their concern. They also did not worry about the fact that when these goods would be needed for a delivery they would probably not be found. Another dissatisfied customer.*

This should not happen in an empowered organization.

The enhancement in organizational performance thus arises from a combination of positive benefits, including:

- improved communication flows
- better decisions
- a more competent and flexible workforce dedicated to continuous performance improvement and innovation
- a more orderly workplace with well-maintained equipment and procedures.

Potential pitfalls

The worst thing you can do is to embark on an empowerment programme without planning it properly from the outset. There are many actions to be taken, people to be informed, programmes to be developed, procedures to be changed and, probably, reward systems to be modified. You must do these in an appropriate order, in a planned manner. Take action in an inappropriate sequence and all hell can break loose. Opposition could be staring you in the face. Such opposition generally arises as a result of misunderstanding or unresolved personal or sectional interests. Who you consult and on what issues must form an integral part of your plan.

> '*The worst thing you can do is to embark on an empowerment programme without planning it properly.*'

Snapshot *We once visited a manufacturing unit where the manager talked loosely about introducing teamwork.*

As in many such organizations, there was one part of the process where a machine acted as a bottleneck. For many years, the person operating that machine had been paid a bonus based on throughput. As a prelude to introducing teamwork, this bonus was removed. The inevitable occurred. He worked more slowly and the factory became less efficient.

There is no point in removing the motivation of a bonus without thinking through the implications of this action. Teamwork has its own rewards and motivations, but it does not follow the waving of a magic wand. This one ill-timed and badly managed decision set the clock back in teamwork development.

Announce any change programme and people are likely to be suspicious and fearful of the future. Because of the climate generated over recent years, any change tends to be associated with redundancies. The argument that improved efficiency – even if it leads to job losses – is good for the organization sounds fine to those who think they will be survivors in the organization, but specious to those forced to leave. It is counter-productive to introduce change in such a way that your best people leave. Your least able people are likely to be the last to leave of their own volition.

In an organization that moves away from a 'command and control' culture to one of empowerment, there is a shift in the power matrix. People's expectations are raised – both in terms of the way managers will behave towards them on a day-to-day basis and in the way they are rewarded. Empowered employees will be using their power in ways that can materially influence organizational success and management will need to trust these people. The people in the workforce are not likely to commit themselves to support the organization if they do not trust the management. Thus crucial pitfalls lie in these three key areas:

- power
- expectations
- trust.

Power and authority

In organizations that become more empowered, managers often feel that their positions are undermined by the fact that their subordinates now make many of the decisions they used to make. They feel a loss of power and that they are less in control. They consider that their roles have been downgraded, that the enrichment of the jobs of their subordinates has led to an impoverishment in their own jobs. Empowerment often follows, or is accompanied by, delayering. The former command and control cultures had a way of building up layer on layer of managers. Intense competition, rapid changes in response to the marketplace and modern communications combine to reduce the lines of communications and layers of management. The question is what to do with the managers who remain.

> *'Crucial pitfalls lie in three key areas: power, expectations and trust.'*

In most cases, the answer is not that difficult. The workforce is left to get on with the job – calling on management and technical support as required. In this context, managers still have the overriding responsibility to set clear goals, monitor the achievement of these goals and create conditions within which these goals can be achieved. Managers will also have the ultimate responsibility to recruit the right people, ensure that they are properly trained, and operate the discipline and grievance procedures on the rare occasions that these will be required.

Managers will now have more opportunities to look ahead, plan for improvements, investigate what is happening outside the corporation, think about the economic and political climate. They will have time to consider their customers' needs and the impacts of their competitors' operations. They will be able to consider applications of new technology, modifications to the goods and services they provide and the skills that they and their people will need for long-term survival and success. They will be able to consider new products and services.

In other words, the empowerment of the workforce offers a real opportunity for managers to lift their eyes beyond the day-to-day concerns, to plan and to take action to secure the future. If managers' jobs are not enriched, they will have a marked tendency to revert back to control and command behaviour. Managers have a tendency to revert to decisions they find easy because they have been making them for years. If they have nothing better to do, they will snatch back decisions that have been delegated to subordinates. Striking a balance is important, but it is not a once-and-for-all decision; it is part of the process that must be managed. The other imbalance that could occur would be that of giving too much authority to people who, for whatever reason, are not ready for it.

One of the fears of managers is that the people they empower may not perform adequately – and the manager will get the blame. They fear that their subordinates may not have the ability to make decisions or commitment to the organization's goals. A manager must make a judgement about the extent to which it is wise to empower a particular individual or group of people. The nature of the work also has a bearing on the extent to which decisions can be delegated.

For individuals, empowerment must always be limited to some extent. The boundaries need to be drawn carefully and communicated clearly to everyone concerned. Overall limits to authority will be laid down by senior managers, but will need to be interpreted at the local level. Even in an empowered organization there will need to be disciplinary procedures to correct and, if necessary, to remove people who are not performing adequately, whether these people are in management or other roles.

In our experience, most workers directly involved in the production of goods or the provision of services will cooperate enthusiastically in an empowered organization. There may be a few people (about 1 or 2 per cent) who continue to do their job properly, but do not fully cooperate in team discussions and suggestions. They pose no threat to progress. People on the front line do not have to be disciplined as a result of the introduction of teamwork or empowerment initiatives. It must be said, however, that some managers find it impossible to operate effectively in an empowered culture.

Expectations

In any change programme people will build up their own pictures of what the future will be like. Once past the fear, doom and gloom stage, people will become more positive. As managers you may talk about informing them more, listening to their views more, giving them more power and so forth. As they start to believe in this new approach you intend to take, they will start to look for the behaviour to match the words. Here is the pitfall: do not promise what you cannot deliver. If you promise information, institute a system for distributing that information, feed the system, monitor it and ensure that it works. If you promise to listen to people, make sure you have a system that feeds back responses to every suggestion made and every question that is asked. Detailed methods are discussed later, here we are concerned with the principle.

'As people start to believe in your new approach, they will look for behaviour to match the words.'

Sometimes organizations consider it worth while conducting opinion surveys where employees are asked to comment on various aspects of the company's style and systems. The snag is that, occasionally, the senior managers concerned have not recognized that such a survey is itself a major intervention – a change agent. The intervention aspect of such a survey far outweighs its importance in assessing people's views. Any competent consultant could find out the key issues and opinions by spending a day doing structured interviews with a variety of people in the workplace. This could easily be a low-key exercise, although it would be wise to clear this with the trade union officers (if there are recognized unions) or other representatives before putting questions to employees below management level.

When you start to ask questions – whether this is in structured interviews or though questionnaires – you raise the expectation that somebody in management is going to read them and take the replies into account in some way. If you ask everybody, then, to an extent, everybody has raised expectations. As management, you need to think through how you will respond *before* you design, let alone issue, the questionnaire. If you fail to respond you have, in effect, said 'Thanks for nothing: nobody in management cares what you have to say'. That may not be what you have said, but it is what people hear. In this business, what people perceive determines what they believe and how they behave.

'In this business, what people perceive determines what they believe and how they behave.'

Remember that the questions you ask determine, to a considerable extent, the replies you get. How often have you been frustrated by a forced choice question when none of the answers offered matches your view? Another factor is the extent to which the respondents take the questionnaire seriously. If people think the survey is serious, the enquiry genuine and that something positive will come out of it, they will complete it carefully – the first time. However, if experience leads people to believe that this is a sop to the workforce and that the results will not be used in a sensible way, do not expect worthwhile replies.

So, the conclusion we can make is that, first, the need for a survey and the use to be made of it must be thought through *before* carrying it out. Second, you need to consider what expectations the survey will raise and how you will deal with them. Third, any survey needs to be constructed and conducted with care, whether it is a written survey or individual interviews or group interviews or on the telephone. Finally, the survey must be carefully analyzed, interpreted and the results fed back, together with information on any action to be taken as a result of the opinions expressed. The people who answer your questions have the right to know what the results of the survey are and what the response of management will be.

Another area of expectation generally aroused by any change in working arrangements concerns rewards. A detailed consideration of reward systems is provided in Chapter 4, so here it is sufficient to say that any promises you make must be seen to be fulfilled.

Snapshot *A new man was appointed to head up a science department in a university. It did not take long for him to realize that morale among technical staff was deplorably low and that this rubbed off on the service provided to lecturers and students.*

On closer examination he realized that the staff had a number of specific, well-founded grievances. They had insufficient space to do their work. In particular, they needed a room to house scientific balances to make up the materials required for classes. There was a woeful shortage of glassware, such that there was not a spare set to enable the cleaning to be undertaken properly between classes. Even their white coats were all old, worn and shabby. Above all, there were simply not enough people to carry the workload.

He negotiated for modest funds to be used to purchase white coats and glassware, and initiated action to investigate the accommodation question and staffing levels. He then called the staff together and said that white coats were on order and would arrive within the week. Glassware was on order and would arrive within a month or two. The accommodation and staffing question was under investigation, but would take time. ▶

As the white coats arrived and then the glassware, spirits began to rise. The technical staff realized that at last someone was listening to their concerns and dealing with them. It took two years for all these promises to be fulfilled.

Building trust

If your workforce regards you as an honest, open and trustworthy management group, you are indeed blessed. You start with an outstanding advantage few other management teams can boast. If you are not in that fortunate position, you will have a lot of work to do, and in this area there are very real pitfalls.

Some managers will be reluctant to be open with their people. They fear that what they reveal may be used as a weapon against them. It is important to recognize that openness is not about individuals, but about relationships. Even an 'open person' will not be equally open about everything to everybody. We are all selective in the extent to which we are prepared to share what we know with others. We are even more selective when it comes to sharing our values, our perceptions and our feelings with others.

Openness is relative and, as with trust, it must be developed between people over the course of time. Empowerment may mean that a new quality of relationship must be forged between people who may have worked together for years. A newcomer presents two related problems. How open will we be with him? How open will he feel able to be with us? Most people will 'open up' in an empowered culture as they see that the information they provide is used constructively. The quality of the people who act as representatives at all levels is crucial. Do they have the ability to form open relationships with people?

'Some managers will be reluctant to be open with their people.'

Some individuals are trusted because they have a kind of 'charisma' that inspires trust. In most organizations this wears off fairly quickly and people decide whether or not to trust each individual on the basis of the pattern of behaviour they perceive. The word 'perceive' is all important in this context. You may withhold information because it is in the best interest of a section of the workforce, but they may not see it that way. Your actions will then be interpreted as untrustworthy. You may intend to reply to a question put to you in a meeting, but simply forget. To you this is simply an accidental omission, but to people at the

'So, how do we build trust?'

meeting who care about the answer it may be seen as a betrayal of trust. We used the phrase 'pattern of behaviour' above, because it is not just one incident, but incidents over a period of time that build up a picture of honesty, openness and trust – or not. Some incidents, however, may assume a very high degree of significance and become virtually icons of trust – or, more often, of distrust.

Snapshot *In a large manufacturing unit, the management sought to introduce teamwork.*

Over the years, there had been many redundancies and reorganizations. There was, at first, a tendency to think that this was just another management ploy, for example 'to make two people operate three machines and sack the third person'. However, the Production Manager had been away from the plant for a couple of years, but when he had worked at the plant before, he had been a supervisor with a reputation for straight dealing. As a consequence, it was common to hear people on the shop floor remark, 'Well, if J. said it, it is probably true'. The confidence in the word of this one manager was a real asset in taking the programme forward. This level of integrity had, of course, to be maintained. Such 'capital' would soon have been spent if 'J.' had been found making a dishonest statement. He was not.

So, how do we build trust? Simply by continuous, consistently honest, open and trustworthy behaviour – by all directors, managers and supervisors at all times. Sounds easy. It is not. That's one reason the change has to be planned and managed.

Progress checklist

Tick the following items when you can honestly answer 'Yes' to the question posed.

Have you identified the tangible benefits you expect from the programme? Have you decided to plan the change programme properly? ❏

Have you listed the likely pitfalls and the steps you will take to avoid them? ❏

Are you and your managers prepared to face the problems of shifting power that occur with involvement and delegation? ❏

Have you thought through the expectations you will generate with your programme? ❏

Have you carefully considered the place of surveys in your strategy, and the need for detailed planning if they are to be used? ❏

Has the top management team the determination to build high levels of trust throughout the organization? ❏

Do you plan to develop policies and procedures that will enable you to manage the extent to which people are empowered and the level of authority that you are prepared to devolve? (See Chapter 3.) ❏

3

Managing the culture change

A step-by-step guide to the mechanics of making the change

- Focus on opportunities and problems confronting the business.

- Commitment to organizational change must begin with the top management team.

- Review your information systems and staff development.

- Review your reward management.

- Appoint a project manager.

- Set out to manage the change programme in a businesslike manner.

Snapshot *Some years ago, BOC Distribution Services – a major distribution company – was establishing its operational network in the UK. It had one particularly demanding customer and it was essential that the operation would run smoothly and efficiently at all times. The company had recognized the Transport and General Workers Union and negotiated a Charter for Human Relations.*

The code of practice embodied in this agreement was designed to ensure that managers and trade union officials behaved at all times in a cooperative and responsible manner. The company also outlined in the Charter its views on employee involvement and personnel practices. At the outset, a survey by the Industrial Society emphasized the need for improvements in communications.

The management recognized that fine words were not enough and, to strengthen the implementation of the Charter, an analysis of learning needs was undertaken and training provided in four phases. The first phase was a general introduction to communications and how the company wanted to improve. Subsequent training was concerned with:

- *briefing groups*
- *group discussions*
- *group problem solving.*

Personal involvement in these training programmes enhanced the commitment of the workforce and reduced resistance to change. The open management style of the company encouraged trust and cooperation, leading to a more economical and efficient service to the customer. Further training courses were organized to take account of the customer's changing requirements, new working practices and legislative requirements. The thrust of the company's action plan can be described in terms of three 'C's: communication, consultation and coaching (including training and development).

Strategic objectives

Involving employees is more than just a change of procedure. It involves a change in management style and in the culture of the organization. Managing change in this context will involve a review of all personnel practices and reward systems.

There is considerable merit in promoting empowerment to tackle what is commonly perceived as being the dominant opportunities or problems facing the business. In the first place, we need to consider the other organizational imperatives. Is there an opportunity to introduce more effective methods or move into new markets? How can this be achieved and what commitment is needed from the workforce to make it happen? Are there problems with sales performance, market share or profitability targets? Why? Is this because of inadequate marketing and sales promotion, or failure to meet customer demands in terms of quality, reliability and delivery schedules? Are manufacturing, distribution or overhead costs excessive? Why? Is this because the people are not fully trained to do their jobs or the company needs to reorganize or people are not pulling their weight or communications are not working properly?

Snapshot *A few years ago, a company making machine parts recognized that computer-aided design (CAD) would offer them very real competitive advantages, but they had no expert in this field and their people had no experience of this type of work. Instead of recruiting an expert, they found an individual employee who had the capacity to learn how to use the equipment and software. This individual was given a special training programme. Together with a small team of operatives, a pattern maker and a supervisor, he worked out a strategy for introducing CAD into the company. By involving the workforce in this transition, management avoided many of the pitfalls of introducing new working methods.*

Starting 'where the shoe pinches' has several advantages. As you tackle these opportunities and problems, any gains translate straight into the bottom line. Senior managers will be prepared to give this time and effort if they see it as a direct contribution to the business and not an expensive 'add-on' programme causing more work without benefits. Workers and their representatives are more likely to believe the initiative is genuine if they see that management actually expects some real gains from it all. The workforce will not be convinced by any soft approach that makes out this is a kind of 'be good to the troops' activity.

> 'Focus on the opportunity or the point of pain to gain commitment to change.'

Focusing on the opportunity or the point of pain has the added advantage that you can set some tangible goals for organizational improvement that everyone can see and share. But beware. This is not the moment to spell out in detail how these goals will be achieved. This is where you start to trust the managers, supervisors and other workers. In due course, you will ask them to work out how to achieve your organizational goals.

Snapshot *A straightforward study of the manning levels required to service aircraft at a terminal will show marked peaks and troughs through the day. In the competitive world of aviation, you cannot permit aircraft to hang around on the airport apron. The various activities that must take place when a passenger aircraft lands, and before it can take off again, have been the subject of detailed critical path analysis. The peaks and troughs are amplified if the staff are conditioned to work to a formula that stipulates how many people do each task, based on such analysis. At one airport, this regime had persisted for years. The management decided to embark on a new and bold initiative. Managers and supervisors were retrained first, then the ground services staff were grouped in teams and trained in teamwork methods. These teams and their leaders were given the schedule for the day and informed of changes due to aircraft delays and similar problems. They managed the workload more efficiently as they were empowered to make decisions and to deploy their personnel in a flexible and responsive manner through the shift.*

If the primary concern is quality, then an empowerment plan can be part and parcel of a quality improvement initiative. If your primary concern is with productivity, then weave productivity improvement methods and problem-solving sessions into your empowerment development programme. If materials usage is your problem and you have concluded that Just in Time (JIT) methods can help, incorporate training in JIT into your training programme. Set up project teams to empower groups of employees to work out, in practice, just how to achieve inventory and scrap reduction. If you consider that the organization's efforts are not well focused you might consider some form of re-engineering.

Whatever starting point you choose, you will need to take into account the human dimension. Many quality initiatives have failed to deliver their full potential because the workforce was not convinced or committed to the procedures adopted. Many productivity improvements have been achieved only with considerable delays and 'teething troubles' because they were obstructed rather than assisted by the workforce concerned. Business process re-engineering fails without commitment. It is in these areas that empowerment can deliver. Top management can and should set the overall goals for the change programme. Give it time. A well-conducted change programme should show signs of improvement within months, but it will not deliver in full in much less than a year or so in organizations of any size.

'A committed workforce can generally make a poor system work better than uncommitted workers using methods that, in theory, are excellent.'

Employee commitment is, in fact, even more important than choosing the best methods. Indeed, it is a sobering thought that a committed workforce can generally make poor systems work better than uncommitted workers using excellent (in theory) methods.

Some of your employees may be at a disadvantage when they seek empowerment at the personal level. This may arise from physical disability or educational disadvantage or it may be the result of prejudice. Racial or gender prejudice can be conscious or unconscious. Your planning may need to include special measures to ensure equal opportunities for such people (some methods you can use are explored in Chapter 14).

Management commitment

It is not enough for top management to be committed to empowerment and its values. Ways and means must be found to involve the next layer of management. A typical way of doing this is to hold workshops first for the top management team, then for members of the top team working with the next layer of management. The purpose of these workshops is to give managers an opportunity to hear what is intended and to comment on the implications as they see them.

The aim of the workshops is to gain the commitment of managers to the process of change, to give them an understanding of what is likely to be involved, and to give them an opportunity to shape the specific objectives of the exercise. Even at this stage it is unwise to get too close to operational solutions. What is needed is a set of hard and soft criteria against which the programme can be measured. By 'hard criteria' we mean such statements as 'following interviews, all insurance advisers will provide written reports to clients within seven days', 'scrap will be reduced by 10 per cent', 'we will achieve 98 per cent of deliveries on time', 'the last bag off the plane will reach the baggage reclaim area within 15 minutes of the plane engine being switched off', '98 per cent of insurance claims will be dealt with within 10 days', 'our average response time for ambulances to reach the incident will be 8 minutes', 'customer complaints will be reduced to 1 per 10,000 deliveries', 'our market share will reach 23 per cent', 'we will achieve total accuracy in our store picking activity'. In each case, there will be a time dimension built into the statement, and markers along the route to achievement.

As you can see, you must work out what you consider to be realistic targets that can be reached by means of empowerment together with other programmes you initiate. Alongside these you will need some statements about 'soft criteria' – ones that cannot be measured with the same degree of objectivity. Statements such as 'every employee will be committed to solving problems that arise rather than looking for someone to blame', 'every suggestion made by an employee is explored and the results fed back to that employee within two weeks', 'appropriate employees are involved in every significant development in the equipment or methods used', 'employees are keen to help in making new ideas work rather than finding reasons for them to fail', 'employees are keen to help other people in the organization in the way that they work, such as in the way materials, information and documentation are presented', 'employees are dedicated to producing quality products and services, and will not let shoddy work past them'.

'You need a set of hard and soft criteria against which the programme can be measured.'

Management requires measurement, and using these methods you can draw up a list of parameters against which to judge the progress of your development programme. These should include hard and soft measures related to your goals, in terms of productivity, quality and reliability – as well as empowerment.

Review of systems

It is vital to examine any systems that impact on people's motivation and ability to operate in an empowered manner. The four dominant systems in this respect are rewards, information, staff development and authority levels. However, it may also be necessary for you to examine the systems you have in place for quality assurance, health and safety and environmental concerns. In a control and command culture, management knows best. Here, everyone must conform to the detailed procedures prescribed, and no understanding of the processes or reasons for decisions is required on the part of the workforce. As one director put it, 'when you come through the gates, you leave your brains behind'. In an empowered organization, however, employees at all levels need to understand:

- what they are doing
- the context within which they are working.

This will enable them to make sound decisions.

This raises a fundamental question of extreme importance. You need to decide what decisions can be made by shop floor workers, office workers, technical staff, fitters and electricians, supervisors, middle managers and so forth. As a matter of fact, these decisions cannot be made at one point in time. At the outset, the scope for delegation may be limited. As the programme produces more and more able, committed workers, more decisions can be delegated to individuals or teams. Some people find it helpful to have a simple framework that they can use when considering authority levels for decisions, as shown in Figure 2. This is another way of looking at the problem highlighted in Chapter 1 under the heading 'Extent of employee involvement'.

'Examine any systems that impact on people's motivation and ability to operate in an empowered manner.'

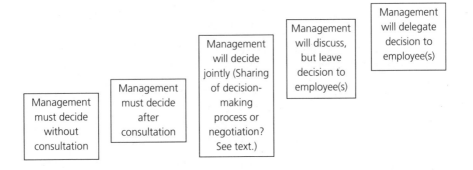

Figure 2 Levels of delegation

Clearly, there will be decisions that management will need to make concerning the future of the business. There may be occasions when commercial considerations (such as a take-over) preclude consultations with the workforce. There are many matters where the management has to reserve the right to make decisions, but where inputs from the workforce could be valuable. For example, many of the procedures for quality, health and safety must be laid down and adhered to by everybody concerned, and the effectiveness of this can be enhanced if staff have been consulted.

Other decisions can be discussed and, hopefully, agreed between management and employees. At one level, these can take the form of negotiations with workforce representatives over such matters as reward systems, discipline and grievance procedures. At another level, decisions about operational targets for the day and requisite manning levels can be agreed between supervisors and teams (other examples are given in Chapter 1).

Managers may not find it easy at first to allow subordinates to make such decisions. Indeed, they will often see this as impoverishing their jobs. At some stage in the proceedings, top management must face the question of staffing levels, span of control and management structure. In a manufacturing unit, for example, the introduction of effective teamwork means that supervisors are not required to allocate work or engage in routine trouble shooting. This is done by teams and team leaders. Often, fewer supervisors are needed, and those who remain have essentially different roles. In our experience, in the past, junior and middle managers have spent much of their time dealing with problems that the workforce could sort out by themselves. As a consequence, they have not paid sufficient attention to the medium-term planning and process improvement necessary to stay ahead in a competitive market.

'Managers may not find it easy at first to allow subordinates to make decisions.'

Empowerment does not apply only on the shop floor. Empowerment on the shop floor means that managers have more time to spend on important issues and, given the necessary training and development, they, too, can be empowered.

Information management and staff development

As with all information systems, we must begin by asking who needs information and how will it be used? Then, there are the questions: where does the information come from, and what is the optimum way to present it to the user? Before the widespread use of computer technology, information was primarily conveyed on paper or by word of mouth. Inevitably, systems evolved mainly:

- to facilitate decision making by managers
- to enable management to account for its actions.

All managers need to account for their management of money and the conformity of the operation to legal and policy requirements.

As decisions become devolved, so information must become dispersed widely, but selectively, throughout the organization: information overload is just as debilitating as inadequate data. Then, people need training in how to interpret this

data, and to make decisions based on it. On a moment-by-
moment basis, this data will primarily relate to the immediate procedure being used – for example, targets, standards
and priorities.

'As decisions become devolved, information must become more widely dispersed.'

However, to operate effectively in an empowered organization, people need to know more about the information
they manage. As we have seen, they need to know where their
information comes from, how the information they provide is
used, and by whom. They need to know what effect their decisions have on the
quality, reliability and value for money aspects of the goods or services received
by the customer. They need to know the effects their decisions have on profitability. There are a number of ways to improve customer knowledge and
encourage customer care. The methods used will depend on the type of business
concerned.

> **Snapshot** *A specialist cable manufacturing company arranged for groups of workers to visit the factory where their products were incorporated into aircraft. This gave the cable workers a sense of the importance of their work, as failure in the aircraft's electrical systems could cause a disaster. Talking to the aircraft workers, they then appreciated the particular properties required in the cables they made. They chatted about the conditions faced by the aircraft in flight, the temperature variations, the need to conserve weight, the flexing of the body and so forth. These cable manufacturing people returned to their factory keen to do a sound job and to ensure that their cable was of the highest quality. Their experiences were shared with other workers at the cable factory.*

In a truly empowered organization, each individual will believe and act as if he
or she owes a duty of care to each person they deal with. A supervisor will regard
his people as 'customers', to whom he owes care and consideration.

> **Snapshot** *An aircraft services department created a video training exercise for its supervisors based on reconstructions of typical incidents on the tarmac. The incidents related to actual problems encountered, such as aircraft delays, faulty materials handling equipment, communications equipment failure, a staff member requesting time off for personal reasons at a busy time. By depicting the problems and frustrations of the aircraft service personnel on the ground, and discussing the consequences of alternative courses of action, supervisors became aware of ways to improve their people management skills. They were prompted to think about maintaining morale and motivation as well as maintaining the quality of service. The aircraft services personnel are, in effect, customers of the supervisors.*

Project management

From the preceding sections it is clear that there is much to be done, and there will be many people to be persuaded. This change programme should be managed like any other project. The managing director must take overall responsibility for the change process. A project manager is needed, reporting directly to the chief executive. The project manager's job is to map out the programme, organize the events and keep track of the various strands of action. There follows a project checklist.

Ten action points

Project Checklist	
1 Gain senior management commitment.	☐
2 Set clear objectives and desired cultural norms.	☐
3 Secure middle to front-line management commitment.	☐
4 Alert the workforce.	☐
5 Develop people.	☐
6 Alter organizational structure as necessary.	☐
7 Review information systems.	☐
8 Review reward systems.	☐
9 Monitor progress.	☐
10 Maintain momentum.	☐

There is no such thing as a typical programme, but there are some key elements common to most change programmes. The order and manner in which these elements are conducted will help or hinder the process. Several elements can be ongoing simultaneously. These key elements include the ten action points given above. Let us look at these in a bit more detail.

1 Gain senior management commitment

This has been discussed earlier. It must be the very first step.

2 Set clear objectives and desired cultural norms

This should be part of the programme whereby senior management commitment is secured. Management commitment implies a shared vision of the future. This can, in due course, be openly shared with everyone in the organization. Be prepared to allow the vision to develop as it is shared with more people. There is a price to be paid in terms of management time and the costs of any surveys, training and development programmes. It is wise to estimate these costs and ensure that the company – and senior managers – are prepared for this commitment. Prepare a budget.

3 Secure middle to front-line management commitment

Once senior management commitment has been secured for the overall vision and objectives, a series of meetings is required where managers from each of the sections think through how this will apply to them. The result is that this generalized, shared vision will begin to take more shape. At this stage, managers need a measure of agreement on how they will behave when the change is underway. It is in these meetings that the thorny subject of organization structure needs to be addressed (see item 6 below).

4 Alert the workforce

It is wise to talk through with employee representatives – in confidence to begin with – the changes proposed and how they might impact on the workforce. If there are to be changes in the organization structure, status and the reward systems, these will be obvious matters for discussion. In some cases, they will be the subject of negotiation. It is unwise to pre-empt the outcome at this stage by entering into detailed negotiations. If there are no serious objections on the part of the employee representatives, this can be followed up by public announcements to all the workforce. This is best conducted in large meetings where the MD speaks and his talk is backed up by written statements of intent. Don't be too precise at this stage. Leave room for the workforce to have an input into the future (the methods for doing this are discussed later). If you are moving from a strongly command and control culture, the workforce will scarcely understand your reticence to set out in detail how everything will work. Be patient. Earn their trust. It is unwise to split these announcements up into small meetings. If the MD has to lead each one, it will prove very time consuming. At a series of small meetings, a variety of questions may be asked and answered – honestly. This means that some people have answers that other people did not hear, with the inevitable possibility that people will see some discrepancy, even where none exists.

5 Develop people

Once the main announcement has been made, it needs to be followed up by intensive meetings where people in groups work with managers. In these meetings, hopefully with a facilitator, people can share the vision, work out what it will mean to them in practice, surface their concerns and find ways to tackle them. People development in effect starts with the top team in their workshop developing the vision. For them it continues as they participate in the workshops for managers, supervisors and, ultimately, the workforce. The development of managers begins in the same way. Special training is normally required for managers and team leaders to enable them to manage in new roles and in the new culture.

6 Alter organizational structure as necessary

The likelihood is that the move to empowerment is part of a move towards a leaner, tighter management structure. This may involve the removal of a layer of management and the appointment of hands-on working team leaders. The remaining managers will have new sets of responsibilities, and probably new job titles. In an empowered, open organization, the way that redundant people are dealt with and the way posts are filled must be consistent. Equity, fairness and openness must be the order of the day. Although the workforce representatives may be involved in discussions about structure, it is usual at this stage for management to make decisions about structure, recruitment and selection for new posts.

7 Review information systems

This review must take into account the computer systems, reporting systems and operational documentation. The key questions are, who will need what information in the empowered organization, where will it come from and how will it be collected, collated and transmitted to the people who need it? Do not fall into the trap of giving everybody everything so that nobody has time to read it all and still run the business.

You should also review – and keep reviewing – meetings of various kinds. Ask what they are for, who needs to be there, how often they should be held, and what decisions and actions should flow from them. Often, as empowerment takes hold, workers will want to meet in groups to discuss problems and opportunities for improvement. Teams across three shifts will want to discuss how to achieve the best results from the equipment over the 24-hour cycle. Team leaders at the outset and part way through their shifts will want to meet to talk about workload and resource allocations. Production and maintenance people will want to talk about how to keep the equipment at the peak of performance. Managers will institute briefings with the team leaders, then team leaders with the team members. This discussion must be kept in proportion, but, as people develop ways of working that they consider effective, the ultimate outcome will be worth the time.

8 Review reward systems

This activity takes time (see Chapter 4). If your intention is to remove payment-by-results (PBR) systems, then the timing is crucial. There will be a window in time when the workforce and management are 'on side' with the changes and ready to work with a will in the empowered environment. Removing the PBR system at this stage may produce a temporary drop in productivity as people learn how to manage in the new culture. It is to be hoped that this will soon be rectified and the productivity enhanced. Delay in reforming the reward system may mean that enthusiasm wanes, trust is eroded and the window of opportunity closes.

'A culture of openness, honesty and trust is a tender plant.'

9 Monitor progress

Provided you have been successful in identifying your hard and soft objectives as described earlier, it should not be too difficult to track progress by reference to these aspirations.

10 Maintain momentum

A culture of openness, honesty and trust is a tender plant. It has to be fed and watered by a constant flow of information and positive action on the part of management at all levels. Thoughtless action on the part of a manager can erode this culture. It is likely to happen occasionally, though, and this will not do irreparable damage. If it persists and becomes a pattern, however, it will undermine the culture.

It is wise to put the key events into a chart using critical path analysis, making sure that you have allowed time for the human adaptation processes to take place.

Progress checklist

Tick the following items when you can honestly answer 'Yes' to the question posed.

Have you aligned the empowerment development programme with organizational objectives? ❑

Are you taking steps towards becoming aware of the knowledge and skills of the workforce? ❑

Have you secured top management commitment to the desired culture and the programme to achieve it? ❑

Will you appoint a project leader and prepare a budget? ❑

Have you a plan to review key systems in the light of the empowerment programme? ❑

Have you identified the major elements in your change strategy and how you will manage them? ❑

Are you preparing policies that will guide managers in decisions about levels of authority? ❑

Have you decided how you will monitor and evaluate the programme? ❑

Rewards and empowerment

Aligning your reward systems to support the empowerment culture

- The sensitive area of rewards must be tackled.

- Reward systems appropriate to command and control cultures may not fit the empowered organization.

- A skill-based payment system may well have a place.

- Care is needed in working out criteria for any merit awards or bonus schemes.

- Changing from one system to another produces winners and losers.

- Non-financial rewards are a major factor in motivating people.

Snapshot *In mid 1992, the management at the 100 year-old BICC manufacturing site at Blackley initiated a major change programme. The aim was to bring about dramatic improvements in productivity within a 12-month period. Almost 25 per cent of the 460 employees were made redundant.*

It was decided that a new culture was needed where teamwork, continuous improvement and empowerment replaced the 'management knows best' approach of the past. Management recognized that there were many obstacles that made it easy for people to opt out of involvement.

One of these obstacles was the reward system. There were difficult negotiations with the trade unions – some 76 meetings in all. The outcome was a new, harmonized, single status package embracing all aspects of pay and employment conditions. For process, craft workers and staff, this meant the same:

- *notice periods*
- *calculation basis for pensions*
- *leave of absence arrangements*
- *working hours*
- *workwear, including the provision of special clothing overalls and footwear where necessary.*

Three separate grading structures with 30 grades in all were replaced by a unified structure with seven grades. The new grades, based on team roles and skill levels, were designed to aid the elimination of the 'it's not my job' mentality so harmful to teamwork. There was no reference in the grade descriptors to specific job tasks. Job tasks were listed separately for reference purposes. The variety of pay rates and components (piece-work, service-related progression, allowances for unpleasant conditions or for deputizing) were abolished and replaced by a single, fixed salary for each grade and fixed premiums for overtime and shiftwork.

The new system raised the payroll bill by 5 per cent – most people were better off financially. There were, inevitably, a few potential losers, but the company agreed to the union demands that these people would be guaranteed their existing pay rates until the salaries payable under the new system caught up. Thus, no employee received less basic pay as a result of the change. The cost reductions, productivity gains and a continuous improvement culture were achieved. The transformation of the reward system was one essential component in the equation for success.

Culture and rewards

The sensitive area of rewards must be tackled. The idea of every worker being rewarded financially on the basis of his or her personal output, as defined by management on the basis of work study data, is deeply rooted and long established in the minds of many managers. The fear is that where such systems exist, their removal will inevitably lead to a loss of productivity. If these systems are removed without a culture change, these prophecies will indeed come true. This is particularly so if there are bottlenecks in the system where high throughput is secured by means of high bonuses paid to individuals at crucial points in the process.

'The sensitive area of rewards must be tackled.'

A glance at Table 1 indicates clearly that in a fully empowered organization, simplistic, individual output-based financial rewards need to give place to a new approach. Managers need to acquire new skills, learning how to motivate people who are no longer 'driven' by the work study figures and the control schedules. It is vital to also take full account of the non-financial, but very real, rewards that come to people working in an empowered organization.

In discussing rewards, two factors dominate. The rewards must, other things being equal, ensure that the organization can:

- recruit the people it needs
- motivate those people to do a 'good' job, at reasonable (some would say minimum) cost.

It is vital to separate these two factors, because what brings people to work for a particular company and to take a particular job may not motivate these people to do a good job when they are in the post. It is worth taking time to consider the motivational mix operating:

'What brings people to work for a particular company and take a particular job may not motivate these people to do a good job when they are in the post.'

- in a command and control culture
- in an empowered culture.

See Table 1. If you move towards an empowered culture, it is essential to ensure that your reward system is consistent with these cultural norms.

A financial reward that encourages an individual or group of people to achieve results *irrespective of its effect on other parts of the organization* is likely to

Table 1 Is yours an empowered or command and control culture?

Command and control culture	Empowered culture
People come to work because they need the money and choose this firm because the rewards are as good as they think they can get.	People come to work because they need the money and they choose this firm because the rewards are as good as they think they can get. They may also be attracted by the keen, friendly working atmosphere.
People do what they are told and work to maximize any bonus going, whether this is for the good of the firm or not. (This means that the firm must be very clever at setting up bonus systems so that the firm gains as the employee gains.)	People are committed to the organization's goals and work to enhance the success of themselves, their team, their plant and their colleagues. (This means that they consider the demands on them to be reasonable, the goals and tasks worth while and achievable.)
They seek their personal fulfilment outside the workplace.	They achieve a significant part of their personal self-fulfilment within the workplace.
As far as work is concerned, they see their self-interest purely in terms of the deal they get in terms of financial reward for the time they spend at the workplace.	They see their self-interest as being tied up with the fortunes of the business. They achieve a sense of personal worth and esteem by succeeding in their tasks, working with others to achieve results, helping others to succeed and being part of a winning team – the organization.
They are motivated by self-interest, influenced by wanting to achieve the bonus – and wary of incurring displeasure that could diminish their earning potential.	They are motivated by a sense of belonging to a good group of people, sharing success and achieving worth while goals.
They are demotivated by feeling like a cipher, and by every perceived injustice or example of lack of consideration by management.	They are demotivated when they feel that they are not being informed and consulted or are being treated unfairly.

prove counterproductive. For example, it is possible to reward an individual or a team for their performance even when they can achieve this by piling up products that the next section cannot accommodate. Such a procedure builds up work in progress, ties up capital and frustrates employees. In some shift systems, it is possible for a team to achieve excellent results by 'cherry picking' jobs to be done and neglecting routine maintenance. This leaves the next shift with difficult jobs and poorly maintained equipment.

It is rarely worth while to promote competition between operational teams. The competition is outside, not inside the firm. What is needed is a culture where teams work together to achieve the best results for the firm. It is vital to ensure that the financial reward system encourages this cooperation.

One of the characteristics of an empowered organization is a considerable reduction in the 'them and us' mentality. Many organizations have found that this can be enhanced by introducing 'single status conditions' across all grades of employees. This means that the same system for payment, holidays, pensions and so forth is used for all employees. Often there is just *one* site restaurant and one car park, with places allocated according to need rather than status. There are still, of course, some variations in conditions, but these are dictated by the needs of the operational processes, rather than a person's job title.

Organizations that have to deal with major variations in demand (for example, retail shops, the companies that deliver goods for sale and many jobbing manufacturers) need ways and means of rewarding people but also of retaining the right to call them in for the busy times. Some organizations achieve flexibility by employing a number of part-time staff. Others achieve it by having their full-time employees on flexible hours contracts. In the UK, about half of all employees are on flexible hours contracts. One system used involves annual hours agreements where a proportion of overtime is available to management 'on demand'. In these systems the issues of fairness and consideration are highly important. People must feel that there are no boss' favourites. If an individual has a genuine problem with being at work to cover a specific period, the way he or she is dealt with will indicate the attitude of management.

A detailed discussion of reward systems is outside the scope of this book, but in an empowerment context, people can be rewarded on the basis of personal skills or by means of merit awards and bonus schemes. There may also be opportunities for individuals to make some choices about the benefit received. In any event, it is important to avoid rigid, mechanistic systems of rewarding performance if the requirement is for flexibility and teamwork.

Skill-based rewards

An individual may be rewarded on the basis of the number of tasks he can perform competently. In skill-based payment systems there is often a grading structure where basic pay is linked to grades. People progress through the grades by acquiring more skills. This is particularly valuable if you are seeking flexibility. In such a system, management must work carefully to ensure that the following conditions apply.

- The grading structure must be considered to be fair by and to all concerned. Notice that it is not enough that it is fair: it must be *seen* to be fair. This is best achieved by involving all concerned (by means of staff representatives and/or trade union officials, as appropriate) in discussions about the system.

- Grades can be fixed by using a system of assessing each individual's ability to perform a prescribed list of tasks. In a particular section these will normally relate to the range of skills that are required in that section's work. In some organizations, the individual may be required to learn a skill in another section as well to gain the highest grade.

- In a grading system of this type it is possible to include other factors when fixing the grade. For example, for individuals who have responsibilities in connection with fire prevention and first aid, these duties can be recognized. Often these responsibilities will themselves have associated skill components.

- The grading system must be supportive of the operational requirements. There is no profit in paying for flexibility that will never be used.

- A requirement to use all the skills must be built into the system. This means that, from time to time, individuals must be required to perform each of the tasks for which they are qualified, and to have refresher training if required.

- The existence of a grading system is not a barrier to the introduction of an element of merit pay or group bonuses.

- If the organization introduces team leaders who are hands-on working members of the team, this role and its associated skills would generally be another factor that would be taken into account in the grading structure.

Merit-based rewards

An individual's pay may be enhanced on the basis of performance and behaviour as judged by management and peers. If there is to be an element of pay linked to merit, management needs to think through the effect of each type of 'merit', the way it is assessed and the effect on the motivation of those concerned. Normally, merit awards would be in addition to basic pay. In this discussion we are concerned with an actual increase in the salary level based on assessed merit, so one-off payments are discussed below under 'Bonus schemes and shares'. The 'merits' appropriate to an empowered organization can include those for attendance, effort, cooperation (in teamwork, in innovation) and contribution to performance.

In command and control organizations it has become fashionable to talk about 'managing absence'. In empowered organizations, the positive approach is to manage *attendance*. The change of word denotes an important change in attitude. The focus is not on disciplining people for being away or arriving late. Rather, it is on encouraging people to attend promptly and enthusiastically, helping them if they have problems with transportation, sickness or dependent relatives, for example. Thus prompt and uninterrupted attendance can be a factor in the merit assessment.

In some cases, these factors are highly subjective. In the past, many such merit-based payments have been based on performance appraisals where the immediate boss determined the level of merit. This was often moderated by the boss' boss, and sometimes by a senior personnel officer. These other people were included in the assessment process to ensure fairness and parity – that is, a level playing field across the company and section concerned. Considerable doubt has been expressed as to the effectiveness of such schemes: sometimes they work, but often they fail to motivate people. The results are not uniformly regarded as fair.

'In empowered organizations, the positive approach is to manage attendance, not absence.'

In an empowered organization, serious consideration can be given to '360 degree assessment'. In other words, merit assessment based on the views of the individual, his or her boss, subordinates (if any) and peers. This type of assessment takes into account the views of those within the section and anybody outside the section with whom the individual has a working relationship. Such an assessment emphasizes the need for clarity of definitions and levels, and is also a sensible way to weight the contributions.

Thus, for a merit payment system to support empowerment the following conditions apply.

- The merit award system will normally be associated with a basic pay structure.

- The merit award system must be regarded as fair by and to everybody and be easy to understand. As with the grading system, this is best achieved by involving all concerned (by means of staff representatives, as appropriate) in discussions about the system.

- The merit award can be fixed in relation to a set of factors. These must be factors that everybody recognizes as being relevant.

- Each of the factors used must be clearly defined and understood by all concerned. This is vital if they are to anchor the assessments to the individual's behaviour to reduce subjectivity. It may be necessary to provide training to help people grasp this concept and apply it sensibly.

- The existence of a merit award system does not exclude the option of having a bonus system.

- The merit award system must be supportive of the operational requirements.
- If the organization introduces team leaders who are hands-on working members of the team, they will have a key role in ensuring that the system supports empowerment.

Bonus schemes and shares

Much care is needed if the organization decides to introduce bonus schemes. Are the bonuses to be paid to individuals, groups of people, sections, sites, the business unit, the whole organization? Probably it will be a mixture. In most cases, very senior people with crucial responsibilities will have their own bonus schemes. If they are seen as inappropriate by the workforce, this will have an effect on morale, but, generally speaking, this should not prove an insuperable obstacle to empowerment.

A bonus scheme based on the performance of specific work groups or sections is rarely beneficial to teamwork and effective collaboration between these groups and sections. It is rare that such groups can achieve results without the full cooperation and support of the groups surrounding them in the organization. It is for this reason that the best unit for a bonus is the operational business unit. This is the unit that needs to succeed. Everyone should share in its success and any rewards that accrue from it.

Some companies have encouraged their employees to obtain and hold shares in the organization. There is no doubt that, provided management takes care to maintain employees' interest in the share performance, this can be a positive encouragement. At first, when the employees receive their shares there may be a period when they will reflect on the way their actions influence the company's performance on the Stock Exchange.

However, in our experience, it has rarely been a key factor in the encouragement or maintenance of an empowered culture. If the company is very large, it is often really difficult for people to see any connection between the performance of the local plant and share price. Even in smaller companies, factors other than plant performance have a profound effect on the share price.

Choice of rewards

In many organizations, the scope for individuals to choose how they wish to be rewarded is limited. There may be some opportunity for people to take pay or time off when they are called on to put in more hours. This time may be taken when the pressure is off or, perhaps, accrued. Senior people may be able to opt for a car or more pay. At very senior levels there are possibilities for flexible reward packages, but rarely can these be applied to any extent at other levels in the organization. Groups of workers may be able to trade off pay for a subsidized restaurant, but as some people will make no use of this facility it is rarely a fair swap.

Winners and losers

Any financial incentive that depends significantly on payment by results involves two related 'reward games' being played out. The financial reward does not motivate the worker to do his or her best for the company. Rather, it motivates the individual to operate the system in a way that maximizes his or her own financial return. This is the first game. If what that person does is to be of maximum benefit to the company, management must set up the rules in such a way that, as the operative wins more cash, the company wins whatever it needs. This is the second game. All too often in the past managers have set up such systems only to find that:

'Payment by results involves two related "reward games" being played out.'

● quality suffers at the expense of output
● over time, priorities change and the system fails to deliver in the new situation.

This explains the fact that many of these systems are changed every few years.

Finally, it must be recognized that any new financial reward system is likely to produce 'winners and losers'. It is the highly productive workers earning a high bonus who stand to lose in any moves towards having a skill-based pay system with merit awards based on a range of factors. Most companies have found that the best way to deal with this is to give such people protected pay for a period of time. In other words, their money is made up to their previous level of earnings, but this top-up is gradually reduced over a period of time. Normally, within two years this top-up has been totally withdrawn. In most instances this is a sensible way to proceed.

Most high earners live up to their income and so the sudden withdrawal of this extra cash could cause a dramatic drop in their standard of living. Failure to make such provision would be perceived as unfair and sour the new initiative at an early stage. Capable people are often opinion-formers and creating a number of disgruntled operatives is not a good start. The cost of these 'buy-outs' should be included in the estimates of the cost of the programme.

Non-financial rewards

It cannot be emphasized too strongly that in an empowered organization positive motivation does not arise from the financial reward system. However, an inappropriate reward system can jeopardize success, acting as a powerful obstacle to commitment. The aim is to produce a financial package that will:

● attract good people to work in your organization
● help people to feel that they are rewarded fairly for the work they do, not just intrinsically, but in relation to other people in the organization.

It is rare to find people who are completely satisfied with their financial rewards – we would all like a bit more. When people perceive that they are *fairly* rewarded, however, they are generally prepared to get on with the job, provided other factors support this view.

'An inappropriate reward system can jeopardize success.'

In empowered organizations, it is vital to look to the non-financial rewards that people gain from the working environment. The art of management in this context is to ensure that these non-financial motivational factors work in favour of the organizational goals. A clue to the motivational factors is provided in Table 1. In general, people are motivated to give of their best when they achieve a sense of:

● security
● belonging
● recognition
● achievement.

In an empowered organization, management must set out to provide for these needs, and maintain the momentum constantly. Here are some ways in which it can do this.

● *A sense of security* can be encouraged by keeping people informed about developments in the business and at the workplace. Few people have job security these days, but people feel more secure if they believe management is not likely to surprise them with dramatic changes that will affect their lives. People also feel more secure if they have confidence in their own abilities. Organizations therefore need to put in place systems that enable people to feel successful, develop their skills and have these skills recognized.
● *A sense of belonging* arises when people are 'in the know'. The ultimate sanction of 'sending someone to Coventry' derives its power from this. We have

effectively disowned that individual. There are several steps that management can take, apart from the provision of information. Involving people in discussions about their work and personal development, their section, initiatives involving new equipment and procedures, protective clothing and workwear – all this helps people to feel that they 'belong'.

- A *sense of recognition* comes about when people are called by their names, when their opinion is valued and their queries or comments are treated seriously. This can be coupled with tokens that emphasize their worth – name badges, personal clothes lockers, smart uniforms (these can be as simple as T-shirts or overalls). The way these ideas are applied will obviously depend on the circumstances.

- A *sense of achievement* can be reinforced in a number of ways. It may be worth while to ask people what makes a day good for them, and what they find frustrating. This will give clues as to how a sense of achievement can be achieved on a daily basis. Achievements are often shared – for example, by the whole section or the team on shift. Managers should seek ways of providing feedback on achievement on a daily basis to reinforce this. In our experience, numbers that go up as achievement improves are most helpful. This is preferable to keeping figures that emphasize failures. For example, it is better to talk about the percentage of deliveries that were on time than the percentage that were late.

Snapshot   *A delivery company was concerned about complaints from customers concerning their drivers. The delivery drivers often appeared unkempt and careless in their behaviour and in the way they entered homes. They did their jobs properly, but did not project a good image, although the vehicles they used were regularly painted and cleaned. The drivers had overalls and two sets of gloves, one set being reserved for rough work, for example moving goods.*

The management of the delivery company talked this problem through with the drivers. The drivers attended workshops where the expectations of customers were discussed. Another of the actions taken was to design a new uniform in full consultation with the drivers, and to consult them, too, about the design of the gloves that they would use.

The drivers took a pride in their new uniforms and were happy to use the gloves correctly. They now felt valued members of the delivery company and conducted themselves accordingly.

It is not surprising to find that where an organization has moved substantially and rapidly in the direction of involvement and empowerment, employees report that it is a happier place to work. Some people even report that they now look forward to coming to work!

Progress checklist

Tick the following items when you can honestly answer 'Yes' to the question posed.

Do you propose to review your reward systems? ❏

Have you examined how your reward system will impact on empowerment? ❏

Have you determined what kind of reward system would be appropriate for your organization? Will this achieve maximum motivation at reasonable cost? ❏

Do you have confidence in the steps you will take to involve people in producing a new reward system? ❏

5

Choosing the approach

Finding the best way for your particular organization to succeed

- Focus the empowerment programme on your organization's needs.

- Consider the quality and customer care approach.

- Empowerment can revitalize your organization.

- Empowerment is an essential concomitant to business process re-engineering.

- Learning and development can be used as tools of change.

- Teamwork can unlock your firm's talent.

In 1990, The Natural History Museum faced escalating costs and restricted income linked to a decline in government funding, forcing the organization to become more financially self-sufficient. Senior management decided to initiate a major internal restructuring programme, redefining both strategic and operational priorities with an aim to modernize and improve. With labyrinthine buildings and a staff of nearly 800, employee communication was seen as one of the key issues to be tackled. The traditional structure of the Museum had discouraged communication between departments. The scientific departments were particularly isolated.

The appointment of its first Public Relations Manager in 1992 heralded a more strategic approach to communications in general and an emphasis on improving internal communications in particular. An employee attitude survey in 1994 reinforced the need for museum-wide improvements in communication and a steering group was set up to oversee the development programme led by the public relations team. This group included junior managers representing key business areas and was seen as a consultative group, a practical task force and a communications network.

The results of a communications survey were fully shared with staff, and this demonstration of openness emphasized management's commitment to cultural change. In the short term, it led to the development of a staff newsletter, an improved staff suggestions scheme and the creation of information 'hot spots' – a system of noticeboards where staff could read and collect up-to-the-minute news.

Another area that needed to be addressed related to the team briefing system – the monthly cascade of information from the Museum's management group to staff. The 1994 staff communications survey had revealed that the system was not working, with wide variations in how the system operated across departments, with 14 per cent of staff receiving no briefing whatsoever.

Workshops were held with 95 managers to revitalize the system and guidelines produced to set common standards. Further developments included the creation of regular 'Talkback' sessions on issues of cross-Museum interest aimed at encouraging more open debate among staff and with senior management.

Greater emphasis has now been placed on communications training, both as part of staff induction and in the formal Management Development Programme. A second staff communications survey has recently been conducted to enable the Museum's communications team to check on progress achieved over the last three years. This, together with the use of the Internet for enhancing both external and internal communications, will undoubtedly have a profound effect on the culture of the organization.

There are several different ways in which an organization can set about involving its people. In Chapter 3, the key elements of an empowerment programme are described. Here we are concerned with the overall approach to be taken and the methods that might be employed (a detailed discussion of methods is provided in Part II). To simplify the discussion we will focus on topics that commonly form the basis of culture change programmes. These include quality and customer care, organizational renewal, business process re-engineering, learning and development, communications and teamwork. A development programme can, of course, involve several of these factors and more. For example, it can incorporate delayering, changes in production methods and the introduction of JIT methods at the same time. If you have people who are in any way disadvantaged, you may need to include special measures to help them to play a full part in the empowerment programme.

Quality and customer care

The usual approach to a major thrust on quality improvement is to start by defining more carefully just what your customers look for in the products and services you provide. Sometimes this becomes a paperwork exercise, starting with customer surveys. These are followed by a few people writing up product and service specifications and driving the exercise through the organization, detailing at each stage what needs to be done to achieve the correct specification. The key to achieving the goal of total quality management is to see that in every activity, people are committed to 'doing it right, first time, every time'. Statistical methods are used whenever these are appropriate. The problem that can arise with this approach is that it is possible to get the paperwork right, but fail to gain the commitment of the workforce to the procedures prescribed – with potentially damaging results.

If you want to develop an empowered organization alongside the development of a modern quality assurance system, start to involve employees in the gathering of information about your customers. Marketing people are often suspicious of the opinions of salespeople, but they are close to your customers – and a valuable source of insights into their needs. A detailed look at market survey methods is outside the scope of this book, but, briefly, in most cases there is merit in considering:

- written and telephone surveys to determine needs as they are currently perceived
- focus groups and expert-based studies to get a handle on the way needs might develop in the future.

By involving your staff in these activities you can begin to build confidence in the process and the need for change.

There is always a trade-off between costs and quality and part of any effective marketing strategy is determining the optimum quality/price formula and market niche for the organization's products and services. Building features into a product when these are not valued by the customer can increase costs to unacceptable levels. This is another factor that must be shared with employees if they are to play a full part in making the enterprise successful.

> **Snapshot** *A company making computer cabinets found that the manufacturing costs were not competitive. As the managers investigated costs at each step, they found that the time taken to buff and polish the metal cabinets was unacceptably high. Further investigation showed that the employees concerned were smoothing the insides of the cabinets to the same standard as the exterior. Although it was clearly essential to remove any sharp edges to prevent injury to service personnel, there was no need to bring the interiors to a high standard of smoothness and polish. Once this was discussed with the people concerned, new standards were worked out that were acceptable to all concerned, and the costs were contained.*

Customer care programmes are another approach to the problem. Here the emphasis is on ensuring that people in the organization are sensitive to customer needs and adjust their behaviour accordingly. As in the case of quality management, such a programme should begin with an analysis of customer needs and wants. Where possible, involving staff in discovering this data is most helpful. Organizing events where staff discuss these factors and what can be done to improve products and services is essential.

> **Snapshot** *A major car manufacturer was concerned to find that customers in one country were buying other makes when they traded in their cars. It looked at the basic specification of the car, its visual appeal and the various add-ons available and compared these with the competition. It could find no obvious reason for people's lack of enthusiasm for the company's products when they decided to change* ▶

their cars. However, it conducted a survey of such customers and found that there was serious dissatisfaction with the way dealers behaved towards them. The manufacturer then devised a customer care programme and insisted that staff from the dealerships attend these courses. The problem was resolved.

Total quality management brings these ideas together and emphasizes the fact that if an organization wishes to present a caring image to its customers, it needs to develop a caring culture within itself. Thus, in this scenario, each employee is, in effect, providing a service to others – other employees, customers and suppliers. People in the accounts office are providing information to help employees manage more effectively, manufacturing operatives are providing products to the next section or to goods outwards, and thus providing a service. Vehicle drivers are delivering goods to customers. The warehouse people who load vehicles for deliveries to small shops, such as pharmacies and shoe shops, are providing a service to the shop staff who have to unload the goods.

The customer may be someone buying goods or delivery services from the company employing the driver, or it may be the goods inwards staff of that company. In a total quality environment, each of these people will be considering how best to provide that service, in terms of quality, presentation, frequency, reliability and so forth, as appropriate.

'Quality management works much better in an organization where people have freedom and commitment to behave responsibly.'

Organizations in the public sector are adopting a similar approach with their customer charters. They now regularly seek customer feedback on their services so that they can be improved. And staff can actually gain more self-respect from the notion that they are providing the best service they can. However, this needs to be backed up by a management that values this aspect of the work and attends to the reward structure – formal and informal, accordingly.

Many people at the head office of a government department provide administrative and policy guidance services to regional and local offices. If the policy guidance is not well thought through or the administrative services are poor, the quality of the department's service to the public will inevitably suffer.

Although many of the current ideas on quality management derive from manufacturing , they can be applied to all sectors of the private and public sector. Such concepts work much better in practice in an empowered organization where people have the freedom and commitment to behave responsibly.

Organizational renewal

The idea of organizational renewal has been around a long time. In this context it is used to encapsulate the process that characterizes organizations working towards empowerment as part of a total renewal. In many companies, there comes a moment when changes in the market, the available technology, customer requirements and the competition mean that a major re-think is required on the direction and nature of the business. The senior management group needs to renew – and probably revise – its mission. The organization's purpose, structure, customer base, product range and services may need to change.

Many organizations in this situation change these factors and only think about involving the workforce afterwards. Yet, such a situation offers a golden opportunity to involve employees at all levels in thinking through the implementation of the new vision. This does not remove the necessity for the top management team to think through the broad vision, but it is more likely to be fulfilled if everyone is working together to make it work – at the design stage as well as at the execution stage. There may initially be a need for confidentiality due to stock market considerations or competitor sensitivity, but once this is past, the challenge – and its solution – can be shared with employees.

Snapshot *A company was confronted with the need to reduce costs and seek new customers while maintaining its quality of service to existing customers. With the help of a facilitator, the Board members discussed many of the changes required and formulated a plan to engage the commitment of its people to coping with the new demands.*

A series of workshops was held, looking to the future. In these workshops, the challenges were outlined and participants asked to work through the implications for their own sections of the company. These workshops involved groups of senior managers, then middle managers and finally front-line supervisors. Participants were allowed to surface their own concerns and suggest improvements in the way the organization was managed.

Through the workshops the commitment to change of the whole management group was secured. Working with the trade unions and the workforce, the cost savings were achieved and, over a period of time, the customer base has been widened.

Business process re-engineering

Re-engineering is a particular approach to organizational renewal that focusses on the key processes that take place within the operation, relating each one to business success. By looking at the organization in a new way, the contribution of each process to business success can be determined. This leads to a streamlining of business processes and the way they relate to each other, avoiding duplication, reducing waste and accelerating the decision-making process. As presented, re-engineering is often seen as a threat by the people concerned and it may be perceived as a way of reducing staff by the back door.

'Where business process re-engineering initiatives have not delivered, this is often due to the failure to deal adequately with the people dimension.'

Where such initiatives have not delivered, this is often due to the failure to deal adequately with the people dimension. It is doubtful as to whether or not this is a sound platform for the introduction of empowerment. However, some of the concepts could well form a part of the overall programme if they are relevant to the firm and its current modus operandi.

Learning and development

When an organization depends on the ability of its people, it makes sense to think through ways to improve their competence (methods for achieving this are covered in more depth in Part III). The current interest in linking people development with business plans (for example in the UK's Investors in People initiative) is not new, but it has become more popular for several reasons. The main reason is that senior people in organizations have come to recognize that the commitment, enthusiasm, knowledge and skill of all the employees are required to make the firm successful in the modern competitive world. It makes business sense to spend any training and development resources you have on helping the business.

There are now sophisticated methods available for the analysis of learning needs, for delivering learning help and for monitoring people's progress. In using these methods it is essential to include measures of organizational performance as well as measures of individual learning.

Linking learning to organizational performance means involving people in determining their learning needs, and this provides a measure of motivation – to perform as well as to learn. Employees at all levels can see the value of such initiatives. All approaches to empowerment involve learning, especially for managers. It is, therefore, very important to see that the training and development plan takes this – and other – new developments into account.

'Generate a hunger for learning as employees are motivated to improve the way they work.'

But you should not be content with such initiatives if you aim at empowerment. There are two inherent difficulties with this systematic approach to training and development. One is that it is all too easy for them to become 'top down' activities. As perceived, provision is made for learning needs determined by management, but the employees are not committed to either the organization's goals or the learning objectives. The other difficulty is that such processes are necessarily time-consuming, especially if there is a requirement to write everything down in detail. In many companies, events move so fast that some parts of the written plans are overtaken by events.

It is far more important to generate a hunger for learning as employees are motivated to improve the way they work. Then, the systematic approach will be welcomed and the learning eagerly embarked on. Furthermore, learning on and through the job itself will become a way of life. The dynamic learning that takes place in an empowered organization occurs in all directions. Employees learn from each other. Supervisors and managers learn from operatives as well as vice versa. Engineers and technicians learn from craft workers and operatives as well as the other way around. Sometimes people learn together as they tackle opportunities, challenges and problems. In creating a learning organization, the art of coaching becomes crucial.

Communications

Effective communication is a vital part of any change programme. It can also be the main thrust of the programme. In almost any company or public body, communications are a problem. It is not really a solution to set up information systems and get data flowing in every direction.

'Effective communication is a vital part of any change programme.'

The secret of success is three-fold. First, get people interested in each other's jobs and problems so that they feel disposed to help each other with information where appropriate.

Second, take care over the way information is targeted and presented. People confronted with reams of paperwork or over-full computer screens will eventually fail to examine all the data carefully. Find out what people want to know and then present it in a format and at a time interval that makes sense to them. Third, feed the system. Make sure that the information is provided regularly and that people have an opportunity to respond with comments and questions. Make sure that all these comments and queries are carefully considered by management and the results fed back to the people concerned.

The Managing Director of a major multinational company was concerned to ensure that all its employees had authentic information and the opportunity to raise questions.

He instituted an annual round of visits to each of the sites. Before the visits, employees were encouraged to submit questions and comments for the MD's attention. These all arrived at the MD's office and his staff set about finding answers. Then, on each visit, the MD would confront the employees and give them a talk on the state of the company. Following this he provided answers to any questions that had been raised that were of concern to all sites in the company. After this, he would provide answers to questions that referred to the site where he was speaking. Questions that were specific to an individual or section were answered in writing. As part of the overall communications strategy, this was seen as a sound example of openness and it helped to generate a sense of belonging to people in scattered locations.

Teamwork

We are all familiar with the way that people working together in teams can achieve so much more than those same people working individually without commitment to a common goal. This idea has been applied widely in industry and the public sector, where people have been grouped into teams and given shared tasks. However, in the context of empowerment, teamwork is much more: it involves everyone in the organization. As with any change programme, broad objectives need to be set by management and these will be discussed, together with concerns expressed by employees at all levels.

It is important to stress the fact that simply putting people into groups and calling these groups 'teams' may not actually lead to improvements. In some cases it can actually lead to a decline in productivity as individuals have been known to 'coast' in this situation, leaving work for others in the group. This is not teamwork. The culture has not been changed and the commitment has not been achieved. Even when the culture and commitment have been achieved, it is possible for one or two individuals to try to use this as an excuse for making less effort. In such cases, but only as a last resort, it may be necessary for management to step in with an appropriate disciplinary procedure (this is discussed in more detail below).

In our experience, organization-wide teamwork is one of the most effective ways to start an empowerment programme. As with any development programme, the starting point is the business need to bring about a change and defining just what changes are required and what benefits will flow. You will recall that in Chapter 2 we noted that one of the benefits of empowerment is the flexibility that arises when people are trained for a range of tasks and have the discretion to use their skills for the benefit of the organization.

It is important to distinguish between teams with members that have largely the same skills and teams with members of widely differing skills. A group of workers looking after a set of machines will have similar skills. A machine operative may work on a problem with a fitter, an electrician and a technician to solve a problem. Their different skills are now required. Different skills will be needed by the medical staff working as a team in an operating theatre. The processes that underpin effective teamwork are described in Chapter 14.

'Organization-wide teamwork is one of the most effective ways to start an empowerment programme.'

As with any empowerment-type initiative, teamwork can improve under almost any circumstances, but in practice there are several factors that can hinder or help effective teamwork. Management may be able to identify many of these at the outset, but it is vital to keep an open mind and recognize obstacles as they are presented. When new obstacles appear, action must be taken to seek people's views. Appropriate action must be taken wherever possible to deal with the obstacle. If no action can be taken, this must be explained, and management must be prepared for the consequences and the inevitable weakening of the initiative. One potential obstacle – an inappropriate reward system – is covered in Chapter 3.

Another potential problem concerns organizational structure. In most situations, teams of up to 12 people work best. In a large team, communications become a problem and it is more difficult to sustain a sense of shared purpose and achievement. If it is possible to divide the work into team-sized units, this will help to promote teamwork, but there will be occasions when this does not make sense. Finally, it is a mistake to believe that simply dividing people into small groups will somehow spontaneously develop teamwork. Indeed, if these groups each become effective teams it does not follow that the operation as a whole will experience effective teamwork. Sometimes these teams compete with each other and become resistant to new team members. Furthermore, there are many situations when the operational team varies in composition from week to week, from shift to shift or even from task to task on a shift.

For these reasons, it is rarely wise to focus on developing individual teams. In an empowered organization, people form teams when they share a common goal. So, the emphasis is on the teamwork concept and on developing people's skills as team workers rather than on specific teams. This means that instead of taking operational teams off for training together, the aim is to deliberately mix up people from different operational teams and areas so that a company-wide concept of teamwork is developed.

As people acquire commitment to teamwork and the skills to make it work, teamwork will develop in an organic way in work groups on a shift, between shifts, between sections, in project groups and so forth. The skills and attributes of effective of team workers may be set out simply as follows.

- They have the ability, together with other team members, to identify the common goal and to agree on a way to achieve that goal.

- They can perceive where praise is due and give it wholeheartedly.

- They have the sensitivity to be self-critical and to criticize other team members and the team as a whole in a constructive manner.

- They have the intention to work constructively with each team member, recognizing each person's strengths and weaknesses. (Team workers do not criticize in a negative manner and do not use other people's weaknesses as weapons against them.)

- They demonstrate a practical concern for fellow members of the team, helping them to develop their abilities, supporting them when they have difficulties and giving praise when due.

- They share in the success of the team and of other team members when they do well. In an empowered organization, a team member will be pleased when another team succeeds because the competition is not with other teams, but with the external competition. In the case of public-sector bodies, the aim is, of course, to provide a better service to the community, and every team should support other teams in that endeavour.

When a group of people that has these skills and attributes accepts a task, it spontaneously forms a team (see Figure 4, page 190). There is no need to spend time developing individual teams. As people work together over a period, their teamwork will become more effective because they know each other better and can interact more effectively, often using non-verbal signals.

These considerations give a clue to the methods to be used. The most powerful tool is the 'teamwork implementation workshop', where groups of people from different departments discuss how teamwork will operate in practical terms, surface their concerns and work on ways to make progress together. (The nurturing of teamwork is discussed in Chapter 14.)

Selecting the method

Once a board of directors has decided that an initiative is needed and the form it will take, steps must be taken to inform all managers. The method chosen will depend on the size and complexity (in terms of the number of sites and sections to be covered) and numbers involved. Any announcement is likely to arouse suspicion and fear. A face-to-face presentation provides an opportunity to draw out some of those fears and to deal with them. Similar considerations apply when the information is given to workers' representatives and then to the whole workforce.

The spoken word can profitably be backed up by written documents, newsletters, house journals, notices on boards. A personal letter can be sent to every employee if the management is seriously worried about a distorted message being transmitted, for example by obstructive representatives. This latter step is rarely necessary, and only comes about if the organization has, for whatever reason, a very sour relationship with its worker representatives. Another method for getting across a consistent message is for senior people to make a video recording that is then shown to every employee, perhaps with a manager in attendance. These methods are, however, no substitute for the spoken word, in person, from a director or senior manager.

'There is no effective substitute for the spoken word, in person, from a director or senior manager.'

Some companies have used the local press or radio to get across their message. This is extreme, and also indicates to friend and foe alike that the company is in the midst of change.

When the directors seek feedback from the workforce, serious thought has to be given to the effect of the questions asked and the manner of their asking. This is just as true of a written survey as an oral survey on an individual or a group basis. Expertise is required to ensure that the questions asked do not, in themselves, raise false expectations or unwarranted fears. The questions should not be biased in such a way that people's true opinions cannot shine through the quantified data. To make the analysis of the replies easier to handle and interpret, a series of questions with forced choice responses is often used. If these responses do not correspond to the likely opinions, the results will be flawed. There must be room for people to raise concerns that the questionnaire does not cover, and sensitive analysis of any replies received in this area.

Large meetings, where people split into groups for a discussion and then each group feeds back its views can be powerful, but they must be managed well. (such meetings are described in Part II). As with all meetings and feedback-gathering exercises, the purpose of the meeting, the anticipated outcome and what management will do about it must be thought through beforehand.

If you have, or intend to establish, regular meetings of any kind, whether these are informal briefing groups or formal departmental and works committees, they will need care and maintenance. They must be fed by appropriate information, and the feedback generated must be dealt with effectively. Inevitably, questions for management will arise from such events and a mechanism for dealing with the queries and feeding back the results must be put in place and maintained assiduously.

In the process of change it will be necessary to set up working parties and project groups. These will generally have a limited lifespan, being dissolved once the challenge has been met or the problem solved. These groups provide an excellent opportunity for management to involve workers who have something to contribute. This will enhance their esteem, build trust and send a message to the workforce that their abilities are being recognized and their voices heard.

Once a culture of involvement has been established, there are various ways in which information flows can be maintained. Information can be disseminated in writing through newsletters, noticeboards, company handbooks, house journals and the local or national press. It may be delivered by in-house radio, via videos, e-mail, electronic noticeboards or by word of mouth. Be assured that if you do not inform people, the 'jungle telegraph' or 'grapevine', alias the 'rumour mill', will spread the word. As indicated above, face-to-face presentations in briefing groups and, from time to time, larger meetings are preferable. Properly conducted, briefing groups led by trained managers are a prime source of feedback. Attitude surveys and suggestion schemes should be used with great care.

Formal consultations are likely to play an increasingly important role in larger companies. Works councils, departmental committees and safety committees all have a part to play in many organizations and guidance on making the best use of these structures is provided in the next section. If your organization recognizes trade unions, you will need to consider how to engage their interest and support.

In empowered organizations, individuals at all levels become more involved in discussions with their boss and their colleagues. These discussions will cover the nature of the job, the equipment and methods used, the individual's performance and learning needs. Some of this will be informal, but there is a place for some structure in these activities – for example, regular appraisals, team meetings, quality circles and project groups.

Initially it will fall to management to make decisions about the methods to be used. As people become more empowered, they are likely to become more involved in such decisions and to make suggestions for improvements in the way these initiatives can be improved.

Progress checklist

Tick the following items when you can honestly answer 'Yes' to the question posed.

Have you identified aspects or areas of the business where improvements will bring real benefits to the organization? ❑

Have you chosen the overall approach you will take to empowerment, and to what extent this will be linked with other priorities? ❑

Have you decided the kinds of methods you will use and how you will involve people in these decisions? ❑

Do you have plans to establish and maintain an effective system of communication and consultation? ❑

Are you confident that you can ensure that all your people are aware of your organization's mission? ❑

PART II

Involvement methods

啓発

Initiating change

More detail on methods to get you started

- Change must start at the top.

- Culture is more important than methods.

- Collecting people's views can change perceptions.

- Top management must unify around an agreed mission and behave consistently.

- Handled with care, attitude and opinion surveys can prove helpful.

- Coaching and counselling are vital components of the change strategy.

Snapshot *A group of directors had difficulty in agreeing on how to improve quality in their company. One talked about total quality management. Another was wary of the ISO 9000 procedure. One did not see a need for a special programme to deal with the problems they faced. It was decided that the group would spend a day out of the office with a facilitator.*

Preliminary interviews between the facilitator and each Board member revealed that people were using the same words with different meanings. The day began with the facilitator asking each Board member to state his concerns and what he felt was the best way to proceed. The facilitator then outlined a simple model to distinguish between quality control, quality assurance and total quality management.

As the day progressed, the Board members came to realize that their aims were the same and it did not prove too difficult to find a way forward that everyone could accept. The company initiated a fresh quality improvement initiative that successfully secured the approval of its customers.

Strategic change

Change really starts when a member of the management group decides that something must be done to improve the situation in the company. He must then convince his colleagues of the need for change. Together, they must think through the direction of change and how it might be achieved. Organizational empowerment is a strategic issue involving a cultural change and so it must be applied to a discrete group of people. Many of the larger companies have an overall policy to move in the direction of more employee involvement and leave the detail to be worked out by management in each unit. In such cases, the management group referred to above consists of the senior managers on site and, typically, change will be initiated by the most senior manager.

> *'Change really starts when a member of the management group decides something must be done to improve company performance.'*

In other companies, the decision is taken by their board of directors and applies across the whole organization. Change sometimes arises as a direct consequence of the appointment of a new chief executive who seeks to bring about a significant improvement in the organization's fortunes by involving everyone in achieving new goals. Often inspiration comes from seeing what other companies are doing, comparing results and how they are achieved.

It cannot be emphasized too strongly that although the methods you use are important, the culture you create and maintain is of far greater significance. Getting the climate right at the top and filtering this down must be your dominant concern.

Data and discussion

Factual data is an important part of the backcloth to any change programme. Information about costs, profitability, sales, competitor pricing and so forth must be collected and interpreted. Much of the information you need, however, is concerned with people's opinions and attitudes. This is particularly true when you are looking at the way your customers behave and the way your workforce sees the situation. You are now looking at opinions and feelings.

Once you start to explore these issues, you enter into dialogue with people and this inevitably raises expectations and invites discussion. In moving towards empowerment, the way you conduct these activities has a profound impact on the whole programme. You must not consider data collection as something separate from the overall change process: it is an integral part of that process.

How does one set about convincing senior people of the need for change and the form it should take? There are several steps that can be taken to initiate change, and the following list is not exhaustive. Many of these activities can be conducted at the same time. Later, many of the activities described below can be used to cascade the discussion to lower levels in the organization.

'Data collection is an integral part of the change process.'

Activities to initiate change include:

- gathering external data
- initiating expert-based studies
- conducting focus groups
- organizing exploratory visits
- using the services of a consultant
- conducting in-depth interviews
- organizing management workshops
- considering attitude and opinion surveys
- appointing a project manager
- setting up project groups
- formulating policy and plans.

Let us now look at each of these activities in turn

Gathering external data

Gather information about how other companies operate. Be careful to choose examples that the people in your organization see as being relevant. If you visit a totally dissimilar organization, you run the risk of people saying 'this can't work in our kind of firm, we're different'. Where similar companies are achieving significantly better results than yours, senior people must take this seriously.

Initiating expert-based studies

In turbulent times, you may want to get a handle on the way the context is changing for your organization. One way to do this is to use a structured method to tap into the knowledge and experience of a group of experts. Only you will know what kind of expertise is relevant to your particular needs at this time. Typically, one might include people with knowledge about the market for your products, the likely availability of premises, raw materials, skilled people, legal problems that might impact on your business, changes in the competition, developments in technology. Some of these experts will be in your firm, others may be in trade bodies, research associations or academic institutions.

A typical way to start the process is to set out a framework and to put down some markers on the left-hand side of a large piece of paper. Ask the experts to comment individually, in writing, on the right-hand side. The initial comments are collected, collated and recirculated. This process can be repeated to further enrich the data. Finally, the results can be discussed by the senior management team. The framework you choose will depend on your principal areas of concern. One useful framework is to group comments under political, economic, social and technological factors.

> **Snapshot** *The Director of a public-sector organization was at his wits' end. The Board could not agree on priorities for staff development. He called in a consultant and, together with senior colleagues, the Director identified some of the key factors that the Board would need to take into account in determining priorities.*
>
> *The consultant drew up a chart listing these factors on the left-hand side of the page, with a column on the right-hand side for comment. The factors covered anticipated political, economic, social and technological changes that would impact on the industry and the business. Board members nominated experts, and this list was supplemented by experts from trade bodies, research establishments and academic institutions. The chart was circulated to these experts who were asked to comment on the factors listed, noting any key dates. It was important to try to anticipate, for example, when it would be possible to trade in certain countries or when a particular piece of legislation was expected. The experts were also invited to add any new factors they considered to be significant.*
>
> *When the responses were analyzed by the consultant, the list of factors had grown. The data was collated and circulated a second time. Finally, the results were collated and analyzed by the consultant. These results were presented to the Board by the consultant.*
>
> *The report highlighted five key issues that were paramount. On the basis of this data, the Director initiated a discussion, following which the Board agreed on a plan of action to deal with the priority areas. The Director now had a sound basis for planning his activities, with the full support of his Board.*

Conducting focus groups

Gathering opinions and ideas by means of focus groups is becoming increasingly popular. This involves bringing people together in a congenial atmosphere and persuading them to discuss the issues you would like to see explored. In a change programme you might, for example, use a focus group of customers to determine their expectations of your organization's products and services. Such data can then inform the direction of change. By involving a cross-section of your own people in this you can embed an understanding of the reasons for change within the company. You can use a focus group of experts to help you determine the way the environment is changing for your organization as an alternative to the written approach.

> 'Gathering opinions and ideas by means of focus groups is becoming increasingly popular. Involve a cross-section of your own people.'

Involving top managers in these focus groups should lead to a common perception of what needs to change. Once the top management group has agreed on the need for change, a series of focus groups with cross-sections of your own people could be a part of the initial process for gaining understanding and commitment to change – on the part of the workforce as well as most of the senior managers.

Whatever form of focus group you use, there are some simple rules to enable you to gain maximum impact. As in any consultation exercise, remember that not only will you gain information and insights, so will the participants. Be careful of the image you project. Make sure the event is properly conducted and that discussions are always positive and constructive. This is particularly important when genuine criticisms are sought – and given!

> 'Remember that in any consultation exercise participants will gain information and insights as well as management.'

The purpose of the event, the topics for discussion, key questions to be addressed, the use to be made of the results and any feedback to be provided to participants – all this must be made clear before the event is convened. Reaffirm these key points at the outset of the meeting. This will enable people to contribute in a thoughtful way and reassure them that the time given up will be worth while. Humour, in moderation, helps to reduce tension and helps people to speak more freely, although no one should feel compelled to speak at these events.

Particular care is needed when cross-sections of the workforce are involved, and where in the past shop floor workers have not been expected to express opinions in the presence of more senior people. A competent facilitator will help to ensure events are conducted well.

Organizing exploratory visits

If you find some really worthwhile examples, take a group of your senior colleagues to see the operation. Encourage them to discuss the practices involved and the results with people on the ground. Later you may wish to organize visits involving a cross-section of the workforce. They will be able to bring back their own insights and ideas.

Using the services of a consultant

On your visits and in discussions with people in other organizations you may learn of a consultant who has relevant experience and the ability to work well with you and your people. If you find the right person to help, she can be involved in helping you and your colleagues to decide on the way ahead. You may be able to find someone within your own organization to perform this role. The individual must be seen as independent, dealing even-handedly with all managers and any other individuals in the unit with whom she comes into contact. She must not side with any faction within the organization – senior management, human resources, production or whatever.

'The consultant should have a clear grasp of strategic planning and the management of change as well as interviewing skills.'

Conducting in-depth interviews

In about an hour or so, a competent consultant should be able to interview a manager and determine the key issues as seen by that individual. A series of such interviews can be used as a method of building up a credible picture of the company. This picture should include the aspirations of top management and how they see these being achieved. For maximum benefit, the consultant should have a clear grasp of strategic planning and the management of change as well as interviewing skills. If the whole management group is included in this interview schedule, the results will prove a compelling basis for action.

Organizing management workshops

Events where a group of managers meets to thrash through various issues are potentially a very useful way to make progress. Such events can also be a disaster if there is not adequate preparation or if the workshop is not managed sensitively on the day. It is a mistake to allow too little time for such an event. If people are to move to a new, agreed position, this takes time. More than one event may be necessary. Preparation normally involves the kind of in-depth interviews described above.

Considering attitude and opinion surveys

The expectations raised by surveys has been discussed in Chapter 2. Provided you are prepared to deal with these expectations, a survey can prove a useful tool to 'take the temperature' and initiate change.

Appointing a project manager

In any management of change programme there needs to be at least one person who is pulling all the threads together. In an empowerment development programme, a senior manager should be formally appointed as a project manager.

Setting up project groups

It is often helpful for the project manager to be assisted by one or two others who will together form a project team (project management is discussed in Chapter 3). This group cannot be held responsible for the success of the change programme – that is the responsibility of the whole top management group. But the project team can organize events and help the top team to manage the timing of key activities. Involving a staff representative in this project team could be most helpful. She could give advice on ways of managing events that cause minimum problems for employees.

During the change, there may be issues that need to be explored in more depth, for example reward systems, communications or shift patterns. In one or two cases, it may be appropriate to set up a working party or project group charged with the responsibility of producing ideas, consulting widely and making recommendations. The timetable for their activities needs to be dovetailed into the programme. Decisions cannot be left to such a project team alone, but it is a valuable way to explore the issues and to collect a wide range of views.

Formulating policy and plans

'A mission statement can provide a clarion call and a theme for the change programme.'

As part of the process of initiating change, the development or revision of a mission statement can help to bring people at the top together. It may also provide a clarion call and a theme for the change programme. This can be supplemented by a policy statement where the key themes are explored in more detail.

A policy statement may describe the purpose of the programme and the desired outcomes. It needs to paint a picture of the kind of place the organization will be if empowerment is achieved. This picture should include how the company will appear to outsiders and the shareholders, as well as to employees. It should describe the director's aspirations for the company performance and its niche in the market. It should outline how managers hope to behave in the empowered organization and what they hope for on the part of other employees. Such a goal is vital for a number of reasons. It gives everyone a sense of direction. As progress is achieved, it can be recognized. People will be looking for and expecting change, encouraging one another.

This may be accompanied by a statement of initial thoughts about responsibilities for communication and consultation – and, in particular, the part managers will be expected to play at each level. It should include information about the methods and processes to be used for managing the change, the training to be provided, how progress will be monitored and reported back to people. Details on several of these points may need to be worked out as the programme proceeds.

Management workshops

One of the ways in which you can prepare for a workshop is to ask those who will be attending to complete a questionnaire. Often it is better to collect the responses and collate the replies before the workshop starts. At the workshop, the results can be presented and used as data to inform the discussion. The questionnaires usually employed cover topics such as climate, teamwork and concerns. It is also possible to devise questionnaires that are related to a challenge that the organization has to meet.

Climate questionnaires

Typically theses questionnaires will have a series of questions that ask each participant to estimate where he sees the company in terms of climate. The items to be included in such a questionnaire may include to what extent people feel consulted, committed to company goals and ready to accept new ideas.

Each participant will also be asked to indicate where she would like the company to be on each item. Collating these responses gives a first indication of the climate – as it is seen by these participants. A key factor is the difference between what people perceive to be the climate and what they want for each item. The items with the biggest difference scores provide a potential basis for agreement on the need for change.

'Often the priorities and perceptions change as one moves down the organization layer by layer.'

In some cases it is interesting to compare the results between different sections or between different levels in the organization. Often the priorities and perceptions change as one moves down the organization layer by layer. Concerns that are highly significant at middle or front-line management level may not be recognized at senior levels.

Snapshot *A climate questionnaire was issued to each of the top 20 managers in an IT organization. The company had two divisions – one dealing primarily with design and the supply of equipment, while the other division provided a consultancy service.*

The middle managers in the consultancy division presented the consultant with a dilemma. Should they each fill in the questionnaire as a member of the 'top 20' group or as a member of the consultancy management team? They were given another set of questionnaires so that they could do both.

The collated results for the consultancy management replies were in marked contrast to the top 20 replies from the same people. As members of the top 20, these managers saw the organization as autocratic, arbitrary and immune to the opinions of the workforce. As members of the consultancy management team they felt themselves to be in a participative organization that heeded the views of employees and kept people informed and involved. Why this difference? The Manager of the consultancy division effectively shielded his people from the autocratic Managing Director – except when they attended meetings of the organization's full management team.

Management expectation questionnaires

Sometimes it is helpful to include in the workshop some activities that are designed to improve the teamwork among the management group itself. One such involves asking each group member to complete a simple 'expectations' sheet to describe his relationship with another team member. Make sure his opposite number does the same. At the workshop, participants then pair up and compare notes in a structured way.

The expectations sheet has a line down the centre of the page. On one side, the participant writes down what he expects of his colleague if he is to succeed in his job. On the other side, he writes down what he considers the other person expects of him. At the workshop, they take points alternately from each other's list. Much of the data will be the same on both sheets. You will be surprised, however, at how often there are two or three substantive differences in perception.

Generally, both parties gain from the experience as it reinforces their working relationship and often highlights one or two areas for improvement. In the workshop, the pairs are invited to share any insights gained, if they wish.

Management teamwork behaviour questionnaires

One of the most reliable questionnaires for this purpose is the self-perception inventory, prepared by Meredith Belbin and described fully in *Management Teams: Why they succeed or fail*. It is advisable to use the services of a facilitator well versed in the questionnaire and its use in teamwork when using this tool.

The questionnaire can prove an invaluable aid to developing management teams. Often when the team roles of the members of a particular management group are listed, there will be gaps. Knowing what these gaps are will indicate areas of teamwork that will need attention if the team is to use all its strengths to the full. In some cases, there are simple 'drills' that such a team can use to develop ways and means of improving its effectiveness.

> 'The self-perception inventory can prove an invaluable aid to developing management teams.'

Concern questionnaires

One of the main ways that you can gain people's interest at a workshop is to focus on any relevant concerns they have. An effective way to do this is to invite participants to score their concerns beforehand in a questionnaire. This assumes that you have a good idea of what these will be at the outset so that you can list these items in the questionnaire. You should invite participants to score the concerns in terms of both importance and urgency. These are not necessarily the same. You must also leave space for any concerns not listed, and hope that not too many unexpected ones turn up on the day.

If you do not feel confident you can identify most of the likely concerns, these can be elicited by means of in-depth interviews by a neutral person – for example, a trustworthy consultant. Early in the workshop, time must be allowed to list these concerns and any others that people raise. Ensure that everyone understands what is involved. Every effort must be made to find time to discuss these during the event. At the end, provision must be made for dealing with any concerns not covered.

Specially designed questionnaires

A workshop designed to deal with a specific problem can provide an excellent vehicle for improving management teamwork and exploring the concept of empowerment in relation to the organization. Topics that have been used in this way include:

- the preparation of a plan to introduce a new, complicated machine
- improving cooperation between production and engineering departments.

If such a workshop is managed well, participants leave feeling that something worth while has been achieved in operational terms and that they have a better appreciation of what empowerment means in practical terms.

Venues and timing

Many managers find it hard to switch off from the day-to-day concerns of the operation if the office or the factory is just down the corridor. Furthermore, if they know the managers are there, staff tend to call on them for decisions they would otherwise make themselves. For this reason, management workshops are often held '50 miles away' in a suitable location. This can be on appropriate company premises, a conference centre or a hotel. The purely business side of the workshop can be dealt with on a non-residential basis. If the top team feels that there is a need for them to get to know each other better, then an overnight stay provides more opportunities for socializing.

The timing of workshops is critical. If the subject is to be dealt with properly, it is unhelpful to break off too quickly. For this reason, it is generally preferable to allow one and a half to two working days for such events. In many operations all the managers cannot be spared during weekdays when the pressure is on to maintain momentum. However, you do need all the managers who comprise the team for the whole of the workshop. Inevitably this means that workshops stray into the weekend.

Whatever venue is chosen, you will need to make sure that the 'internal geography' is appropriate. Rooms must be light and airy as dark stuffy rooms do not assist animated debate. If you use syndicate rooms, they must be nearby. Time must not be wasted shepherding people from place to place and searching for stragglers. The organizer must think through all the equipment that will be needed and ensure that it is provided. The catering arrangements must be spot-on, all through the event. Good food, hot coffee, on time, every time is the order of the day. Attention to such details is vital to ensure success.

Content and conduct

If you take managers away from their normal work – especially if this is in their own time – they will want two things above all. They will want to be sure that the event is necessary and worthwhile. They will want decent surroundings and good food. The organization must be sound – in terms of what is to be discussed and the way it is handled. Each manager must feel that she has had an opportunity to put across a point of view and that everyone else has considered that observation.

'Managers want to be sure the event is necessary and worth while.'

Although it is important to avoid going round in circles, it is counterproductive to suppress what appear to be unwelcome points of view. They must be brought out into the open and squarely faced. It is all too easy to surface problems and argue interminably. The aim is to surface *all* the relevant problems and seek a constructive accommodation. This is where the skill of the facilitator is essential. The event must have a focus and, hopefully, the end product will be an agreement to proceed and a timetable for action.

Conducting a survey

Use the checklist below to ensure that your survey is conducted in a competent manner, avoiding the pitfalls outlined in Chapter 2.

Things to think about when conducting a survey include:

- its purpose
- its coverage and frequency
- how it is conducted
- its confidentiality
- pre-briefing the participants
- data collection
- its questions
- its pilot
- its implementation
- evaluation of the results and response.

A brief look at each of these points now follows.

Its purpose

If you wish to conduct a survey, first determine the purpose of the survey. Remember that, as well as generating information about what people say they think about various issues, you are making a statement. This statement is that you are interested in the subject matter of the survey, in what people think about it, and you expect to act on the results.

Be particularly careful about the title printed at the top of any documentation. This gives a message straight away. It will influence people's thinking as they read the remaining text. Be careful to avoid words or phrases that can be easily misunderstood. Make sure that all your managers fully understand the purpose of the survey and how the results will be used. You cannot afford mixed messages to emerge because some managers have not been fully briefed.

Coverage and frequency

The purpose of the survey will indicate who is to be included. In developing a change programme it is sometimes useful to survey senior managers, then middle and front-line managers before surveying the whole workforce. You may wish to include only permanent staff or to extend coverage to all employees.

You must not hold surveys too often. About two years is a healthy interval. You will need a compelling reason to hold another survey sooner than this. Once a survey is completed, you need to analyze the results, feed them back to the group concerned, decide what action to take in response, take the action and wait for the outcome. The results of your actions will take time to filter through the system.

How it is conducted

In a change programme, the survey needs to be managed by the project leader. However, each survey is a highly technical and time-consuming activity. The project leader will need help and the analysis must be seen to be independent of management, conducted by some independent people.

The simplest method is to employ an outside agency to help you prepare the questionnaire and to collect and collate the responses. The two commonest methods for conducting surveys are the written questionnaire to be completed by everyone in the group and face-to-face interviews with individuals or groups of people. Some people have tried to conduct such surveys over the telephone.

Its confidentiality

If you want honest answers, it is generally necessary to ensure that specific replies cannot be attributed to individuals. This level of confidentiality is usual in, for example, employee attitude surveys. This is particularly true where sensitive issues such as working conditions are the subject of the surveys or people are being asked to comment on management style. In managing change, however, it is sometimes helpful to mix up groups of people from different levels and different departments in group interviews. The downside is that some people may not feel free to express an opinion. The gain is that by listening to individuals speaking from different perspectives, people start to understand where others are coming from. As an intervention tool this method may be helpful, although the data generated will be less reliable.

Pre-briefing the participants

If you want meaningful answers, make sure the questions will be understood by the people who are answering them. This may mean that some preparation is necessary in terms of briefing people. Be sure that the briefing method you use is sound. Explain why the survey is being conducted and how the results will be used. Include explanations of any relevant proposals in the pipeline. Remember that openness and honesty must characterize the event.

Data collection

The use of written questionnaires can be quicker than interviews and everyone can be included. They are particularly useful if forced choice questions can be used for most of the points to be covered. There must be a space for individuals to add their own comments, although this data can be difficult to collate.

Interviews can be richer than written questionnaires in terms of the attitudes that can be inferred, but they can be time-consuming and the results difficult to collate. You are also highly dependent on the expertise of the interviewer.

Its questions

The questions to be posed – in writing or by the interviewer – must be clear, unambiguous and comprehensive. You may wish to include questions that enable you to verify whether or not the briefing has secured an appropriate level of understanding. Take care that the questions are not discriminatory and that they do not limit choices to what you want to hear.

Its pilot

If large numbers of people are involved, it is valuable to ask a small sample of people to complete the written questionnaire or be interviewed before it is used widely. This will enable you to see how long the process takes, whether or not the documentation is clear and the method is appropriate to the group. Any points that arise can then be taken into account before the main survey begins.

Its implementation

Once the method has been piloted, it is important to conduct the survey as expeditiously as possible. Time must be allowed for people to return from leave, but otherwise do not allow delays. Ensure that you have the resources to see it through quickly.

Evaluation of the results and response

'The results of the survey – for good or ill – should be given to all the people who answered the questions.'

It is permissible to delay the publication of the report for a few days while management moves quickly to evaluate the impact of the results and decides what actions to take. But then the results of the survey – for good or ill – should be given to all the people who answered the questions as well as to the management group. In seeking to build up an empowered organization, openness, honesty and trust must be demonstrated.

Coaching and counselling

If the change in the management style is significant, the senior managers may need some training. Apart from any formal training, one of the powerful tools for change is the peer pressure managers in the group can exert. Managers often see each other in action. If a real team spirit has been generated within this group, the members should be ready to help each other – and to be helped. If the managers concerned have some training in coaching and counselling skills, they can be more effective in this mutual support activity (see also Chapter 12).

If the managers have a clear 'code' of behaviour to which they are all committed, then they can help each other to behave more in line with this code. This is sometimes referred to as co-coaching or co-counselling. As managers grow in confidence and competence, they will be able to coach and counsel their own subordinates and propel the programme forward. This kind of activity will help to create a learning, developing culture dedicated to continuous improvement.

Some people see coaching and counselling as being the same. We consider that coaching is helping another person to acquire some knowledge and skill that you possess, whereas counselling is helping someone make decisions about the way he will behave in future. The two roles are often interwoven in a discussion between two people, but recognizing the distinction helps coaches to be more effective.

Progress checklist

Tick the following items when you can honestly answer 'Yes' to the question posed.

Are all the members of the top management group convinced of the need for change? ❑

Have you decided what steps you intend to take to seek agreement in the top management group concerning the need for change, the direction of change and the methods that might be used? ❑

Have you considered what use you will make of management workshops? What action will you take to get one going? ❑

Have you decided to conduct any surveys? If so, how will you set about this? ❑

Do you intend to use coaching and counselling to help create a learning culture? ❑

7

Working relationships

How to get the roles and structures right

- Empowered work groups will make different demands on management.

- Organizational structures and reporting relationships will need to be revised.

- New communication and decision-making procedures will be required.

- Empowerment means new roles for managers, team leaders and team members.

- Empowered organizations can have an impact on the people with whom they do business.

Snapshot
A production department employing some 300 people was organized into 6 sections. Most of these workers were machine operators, but a number of fitters and electricians also worked alongside the operators, reporting to the engineering supervisor on shift. Working in shifts, each section was managed by a production supervisor and two charge hands on each shift.

There was one overall department manager with a deputy. Thus, there were numerous production supervisors, a few engineering supervisors, many charge hands and two managers. When the decision was made to move towards teamwork and empowerment, the plant was divided operationally into more sections, with a manager for each section. Each new section manager was expected to take a more strategic role in improving performance. This manager would work days only, but would be on call 24 hours a day. (In practice, section managers were very rarely called at home – only when there was a real emergency.) In each section, there would be one or two 'teams' per shift, each with a team leader.

The resulting organization chart showed one department manager, plus section managers and team leaders. Engineering support was provided as required in addition to the electricians and fitters allocated to the production department. It was tempting simply to change the titles of the people in the posts. However, a job and person specification was prepared for each of these new posts and people recruited against these criteria. Those who failed to find jobs in the new set-up were dealt with sympathetically.

New relationships had to be forged to make the new organization work. There was a need for better cooperation between teams on shift and between teams across shifts and a new sense of the ownership of the equipment was fostered. Together with other measures, the structure proved highly successful after some initial teething problems.

People form new working relationships as an organization moves towards empowerment. New ways of managing information and decisions are required. You need to think through what is likely to be the pattern of command, how resources will be allocated and where information will need to flow. Before discussing particular methods, it is useful to think about the structures and working relationships that develop in empowered organizations. People with new roles will need new skills.

Empowered work groups

In a command and control structure, information normally reaches work groups via the supervisor and, where appropriate, computer or paperwork information systems. The supervisor will tell the group what work needs to be done and will allocate the work to individual members of the group. She will monitor progress and quality, reallocating work and people as required through the shift. She will move in quickly to resolve any problems that arise. The information provided by computers and documentation will provide data on the work to be done, specifications and the like. The worker is trained to do the tasks allotted, and not expected to question the methods, the work allocation or the priorities for action.

'Command and control methods fail to harness the full potential of the workforce, and improvements in working methods are often hard to win.'

In a well-run organization, such systems can produce satisfactory results. Success depends on well thought out systems and methods, coupled with consistency and fairness on the part of managers. A hard taskmaster, if consistent and fair, will command a measure of respect and commitment to the work. But the command and control method fails to harness the full potential of the workforce, and improvements in working methods are often hard to win.

In an empowered organization, people at the sharp end often work in teams. When the team members arrive on shift they will look at the information provided, choose the equipment they will use, decide which team member will do each task and get on with the job. In some cases, the team leader may need to confer with other team leaders, for example, if there is a need to reallocate team members to other teams due to absences or workload imbalance. From time to time, the team leader will receive information from his manager and will wish to pass that on to team members, usually at the beginning of the shift. There will also be matters raised by the team members that need to be passed to the manager.

When a team encounters a problem it cannot cope with, a team member will seek appropriate help. This might be from an electrician, a fitter, a technician, another team, from production control personnel or from an IT technician familiar with the software being used. (In a command and control structure, such help would be sought from the supervisor.) The team member goes directly to the person or section concerned. The team member who seeks assistance will often be the team leader, but not invariably.

It can readily be seen that in this scenario there is no need for operational contact between the supervisor or manager and team members every day or on every shift. The manager's role is no longer that of an overseer, allocating tasks and dealing with problems. He must set the goals and monitor the outcomes. The manager must be the one to deal with a discipline problem that cannot be handled unofficially by the team members. In an empowered culture, many potential discipline problems are dealt with by team members and the team leaders themselves – before they become serious enough to warrant official action. Team members will help the individual to cope with his problem and only refer the matter to the manager if the individual will not be helped. The emphasis is on helping the individual to succeed in his job.

The manager is also responsible for recruiting and selecting her people. The extent to which team members and team leaders are involved in this process often evolves over a period of time. It is unwise to try to specify this too precisely at the outset.

The prime responsibility of the manager is to provide the right context for his people to succeed. This means paying close attention to working conditions, equipment, methods, training and development. All these matters will involve discussion with team members. The manager must look ahead, take an interest in the marketplace, competitor activity, sources of supply of materials and developments in technology. She must also walk the job – not to interfere, catch people out or find fault, but to take an interest in people, listen to their ideas, encourage them in their successes, take the pulse of her part of the organization.

Empowered structures: consultation and negotiation

Empowered organizations tend to have fewer layers of management. Managers have less of a role in the day-to-day supervision of work. The focus for management must become more strategic and forward-looking. In an empowered organization, the role of management is to provide the context and environment for the workforce to succeed.

Employee involvement and empowerment can occur at different levels and involve different groups of people. The choice of method will depend on your objectives, the level of involvement and size and nature of the group of people concerned (see Table 2). The choice of method will also depend on the extent to which directors and managers wish to engage with other employees. Examples of the levels of involvement in the decision-making process that can occur are described in Chapter 1. These levels include informing people, consulting with people, sharing decisions, delegating and negotiating.

Table 2 Empowerment matrix

	Informing people	Consultation and two-way communication	Formal consultation	Shared or delegated decision-making	Negotation
Individual level					
Work groups and project groups					
Representational structures					
Multidirectional					

Informing people means letting people know what is happening to the business. For example, in terms of the business and political environment, broad business plans, plans for the unit where they work, envisaged changes in working practices and so forth (see Chapter 8). The trick is to optimize the level of information, the timing and the presentation. People become bored very quickly and their interest needs to continue to be stimulated.

Sometimes you cannot share information with everyone. The question is not what can we tell the troops, but what can we *not* tell them. In an empowered organization, management must ask what information must not be disclosed and why and for how long. Confidential information must be kept to a minimum and remain confidential for the shortest possible time. As management earns the trust of the workforce, the keeping of an occasional secret, for good reason, will be accepted.

Consulting people involves two-way communication – inviting people to give their views and asking questions, but with no specific commitment to act on opin-

> 'Levels of involvement include informing people, consulting with people, sharing decisions, delegating and negotiating.'

ions expressed (see Chapter 9). There is an expectation that management will at the very least consider the views expressed before making a decision. Indeed, it is patently dishonest to consult with people about a decision that has already been made. In practice, the situation is that a general policy decision has been made – and announced – and the consultation is about matters of implementation yet to be decided. For example, management may have to cut costs. This can be announced, followed by consulting people about how best to achieve these savings with minimum disruption to the business and with measures to reduce the impact on vulnerable individuals.

Two-way communication involves more than consultation. It includes encouraging people to make suggestions about matters that have not been raised by management (see Chapter 9). In *formal consultation*, typically representatives are informed about plans at a formative stage and views are sought. There is an implicit understanding that, where possible, these views will be taken into account before final decisions are made. In this process it is very important to be clear about just what has been decided beforehand, and what is left to be decided where comments can be taken into account.

Sharing or delegating decision making means giving people more control. People are allowed more freedom of action within specified limits, giving them the authority to make decisions and holding them accountable for the results. Involving people in decisions where there is a distinct difference of view about what should happen becomes *negotiation*. Such differences of view often arise because there is a difference of interest. What is an advantage to one person or group may be seen as a disadvantage to another party involved (see Chapter 10).

Within a given organization, the level of involvement may change from topic to topic. It is vital to be clear about the level of involvement in each case, to be consistent and to provide adequate feedback. A further distinction must be made between 'representational' involvement and 'individual' involvement.

As noted above, when two individuals or groups of people need to work together, but have different interests, negotiation is required. This may be quite informal. Two fitters in an empowered organization were talking about their workload one day and one was heard to say, 'If I tackle this job, will you do that one?' The other replied: 'Yes, that's OK'. This kind of give and take negotiation is going on all the time in everyday life.

At other times, of course, the negotiation can be much more detailed. Negotiations between buyer and vendor are commonplace. If the negotiation is concerned with employment terms and conditions, these may involve formal negotiations with employees' representatives, often trade union leaders. Advice on negotiation methods is provided in Chapter 10.

New roles for old

Individual empowerment occurs when decisions are effectively shared or delegated to individual employees – and they accept the responsibility. On the 'shop floor' many decisions can be delegated if the worker concerned:

- understands the requirements of the firm, the information, priorities and parameters involved
- has the ability to make these decisions
- is committed to the organization's goals.

The team member's role thus becomes far more proactive. The kind of team leader required and the extent to which responsibilities are delegated to that individual depends on the particular organization. One method is to regard the team leader as a working member of the team who has some extra responsibilities concerned with communicating with management and other teams on behalf of his own team. Typically he will also have responsibilities for coaching, counselling and encouraging other team members.

However, he should not be made responsible for the performance of the team. That responsibility is shared by the whole group of people who comprise the team. He should not be made responsible for discipline. Initially that is also the responsibility of the whole team. Ultimately the manager may have to step in and initiate formal disciplinary procedures.

It is important to recognize that empowering the front-line workers means potentially impoverishing the role of the managers concerned. In many organizations this involves actually replacing two layers of management with one layer of management plus hands-on, working team leaders. The role of each manager who remains becomes more strategic, as described above. During the transition period this may mean that the roles of charge hands and supervisors disappear, as the roles of managers change. It may be necessary to select the new managers and team leaders, from all three groups – and from the shop floor.

'The team member's role becomes far more proactive.'

Those team leaders selected from among the charge hands (and possibly supervisors) will need to be trained to operate effectively in the new culture. It is as if you have taken away the tool set they are accustomed to using in their people management. You have to provide them with a new tool set and train them to use the new tools. A clue to the new tools is provided in Table 1, page 48. Similar training will be required for the 'new' managers. Most of these will be drawn from the ranks of the existing managers and supervisors.

Empowered organizations have an impact on the other companies with whom they do business. This subject is explored in more detail in Chapter 11.

Progress checklist

Tick the following items when you can honestly answer 'Yes' to the question posed.

Have you considered the way you expect work groups to manage on a day-to-day basis? ❑

Do you have a plan to provide management support and appropriate services to work groups? ❑

Have you discussed within the management team the extent to which it is appropriate, in your organization, to involve people in decision making? ❑

Does every manager recognize the essential difference between consultation and negotiation? If not, what will you do about this? ❑

Do you have a method for choosing which topics to disseminate information and/or initiate consultations about? ❑

Have you decided in what areas delegation and sharing in decision making will be helpful? ❑

Have you identified the areas where negotiation will be required? ❑

Informing people

Effective methods for disseminating information

- Support empowerment by producing effective written communications.

- Set up regular face-to-face communications and 'feed' these events with information.

- Major changes may be communicated by means of special events.

- Do not forget the importance of person-to-person contacts.

- Manage communication with work groups and project groups.

- Prepare to cope with information flows in every direction.

> **Snapshot** *A medium-sized company with a head office and seven operational units decided to introduce a communication system throughout the whole organization. The company recognized one trade union and discussed their ideas with them.*
>
> *The company set up department and site committees with elected representatives from the workforce and local managers as members. They also set up a company-wide council where representatives of the workforce could meet up with the Managing Director, other directors and senior managers. For several years the system worked well. Management provided regular information and was sensitive to issues raised by the workforce.*
>
> *After a while, however, management became aware of the fact that, although the meetings were still being held, they had become mechanical and failed to excite the interest of the workforce. A fresh initiative was launched to revitalize the system, beginning with training workshops for managers.*

Effective communication is an essential condition for managing change and supporting an empowered culture. People who are 'in the know' tend to feel more strongly committed to the organization's goals. In almost any company or public body you will find that employees complain about lack of information. They never seem to get enough. Yet, providing this information in an attractive form to maintain interest is not that easy. Managers need discipline to maintain the information flow. Methods for generating feedback are covered in the next chapter.

Regular written information

First of all, it is useful to find out what information people would like to have and how often. You must get past the common cry 'we want to know everything!'. When the chips are down, there are simply not enough hours in the day to tell everybody everything all the time. Typically, people want to know in general terms how the business is performing. Reporting on this monthly is adequate in most cases. They would also like to know how their particular unit stands in terms of future prospects – for example, how full is the order book? Public-sector employees will be interested in impending legislation that could affect their workload and the structure of their departments. People are keen to know about any likely changes in job content or organizational structures due to changes in products, services or technology. This is all fairly general material that can be produced at company and plant level, but also ask people what information they would like to have.

'People like to know the results of their work.'

In many organizations it will be helpful to provide more information about new customers or new types of orders. This will help people to feel involved and more responsible towards their customers. If the company has several orders or projects in progress at the same time, information about priorities will be of interest. Some of this information may be specific to the particular unit or section. People also like to know the results of their work. If your company is striving to improve delivery performance, for example, regular information on this topic should be provided.

Remember, however, that some people may need help in understanding parts of this information. Many employees do not know what effect their actions have on productivity or profit. Some do not realize the relationship between profit and investment. To make the information process effective, you will need to take this into account when deciding on which method of presentation you will use. In some cases, it might be helpful to provide some simple training to help people to benefit from this data. Much of this could be accomplished by means of short sessions in briefing groups (see below).

Snapshot *A company wanted to involve its employees in the fight against waste and inefficiency. The managers realized, however, that many employees had little understanding of the structure of a business, fixed and variable costs and how profit was calculated.*

To start a process of education, a workshop was organized involving trade union representatives and managers. A consultant led the workshop, taking the group through these basic ideas, and the group discussed them in terms of the actual situation in the firm.

The focus was on decisions that supervisors and people on the shop floor could make, especially decisions that had an important bearing on profitability. As these ideas were disseminated, people throughout the unit became more conscious of the impact their actions had on the viability of the firm. Profitability improved. It is now easier to manage change and to make improvements.

In addition to general information, people will be interested in local issues, people in the firm, performance and prospects. Here is a checklist of some of the main methods used.

The methods used to convey information include:

- newsletters
- noticeboards
- briefing groups
- videos
- 'mass meetings'
- company handbooks
- employee information notes
- house journals
- departmental bulletins
- individual letters to all employees
- information points
- e-mail
- company annual reports
- electronic noticeboards
- in-house radio
- local and national press and other media.

A common method of keeping people informed is a newsletter or house journal. The size of the publication and how 'glossy' it is will depend on the company and the number of copies of the publications required. An overly-elaborate publication will seem a waste of money – not the right image in a cost-cutting situation. If a large number of employees is to be covered, the cost may be justified. On the other hand, a scruffy, duplicated sheet will diminish the importance attached to its contents.

A well-presented house journal covering a number of units will serve a useful purpose, but this may need to be supplemented by a newsletter for the individual units. The newsletter will contain information specific to the units that may not be of interest elsewhere. Every effort must be made to produce this information in a timely manner. Too much old, stale news will cause a fall-off in the attention paid to the document. Although such documents provide a vehicle for management to put across its ideas, a measure of independence for the editorial team is desirable. One way to achieve this is to engage a freelance editor.

Employees should be able to submit letters, articles and photographs for publication. If the organization recognizes trade unions or has representatives elected to works councils or committees, they could contribute to the journal. Human interest stories will make the journal more readable and user-friendly. Reports about the hobbies of employees and any honours or distinctions they receive – captain of the rugby team, chairperson of the golf club, county swimming champion – will enhance interest. Variety of content is vital to maintain interest. Even then, you will find that a significant number of people will not read such journals all through and key messages may be missed.

'Human interest stories will make a house journal more readable.'

New employees may be given company handbooks and the presentation and the information they contain is important. If these are in loose-leaf form, they can be updated and this will help to maintain interest.

Many organizations now provide noticeboards where news items and information can be posted. Some managers pin up the minutes of committee meetings on these boards and departmental bulletins can be posted. They can end up covered in dust. The problem with any notice or poster is that it quickly becomes part of the background. If you have such noticeboards, someone must be deputized to keep changing the items and layout, maintaining tidiness and cleanliness, and making them attractive.

In addition to pin boards, some firms have white boards where comments can be written up with a marker and easily erased. This is particularly useful for transient information. For example, employees on one shift can leave messages about production and equipment for those who follow.

Regular information can also be presented electronically, for example using an electronic noticeboard or via the computer system. If your employees all have ready access to computer terminals, information can be presented via this medium. This may also be useful if you have people working away from the office, for example salespeople, who regularly plug in their computers to headquarters for updates. However, unless there is a discipline that requires people to consult these computers on a regular basis, it will be easy for many people to miss key data.

There are devices that will display information in a streamer form. Such data can usually be quickly updated. It can be used, for example, to inform people about events as they occur. This could include information about visitors, productivity levels, delivery performance and the like. As with any permanent presentation device, variety is essential to maintain interest. If it becomes unduly repetitive it will fade into the background and be ignored.

All the above methods require people to read the material provided. A more stimulating approach is to prepare a video presentation, but this is rarely worth while on a regular basis. The logistics of viewing for all the employees may be difficult and expensive to arrange.

Regular face-to-face briefings

Written information, however well presented, is no substitute for face-to-face contact. It is for this reason that the idea of 'briefing groups' has become so popular. Put simply, a briefing group draws together a small number of people so that one individual can talk to them, provide information and seek to deal with any queries about the data provided. Briefing groups with a wider brief, including the generation of ideas and feedback, are covered in the next chapter.

Commonly, a basic briefing document is prepared by the top management group and each senior manager briefs the group of managers who report to her. The senior manager may add to the brief any information that is specific to her department. Then, each of these middle managers briefs the supervisors or team leaders who report to them. The process is cascaded down until finally the team leader or front-line supervisor briefs the shop floor people in their charge. At these levels, this activity may be called 'team briefing'.

'Written information, however well presented, is no substitute for face-to-face contact.'

For this system to work, the brief must be carefully prepared and supplemented by notes on any questions that might arise. These notes will generally be concerned with explanations of any points that individuals might find difficult to understand. The notes may contain more background information for those who may not know the circumstances. The essence of effective briefing is giving the same message to everybody. Those who do the briefing must not embellish their answers with 'extra' information or personal interpretations. We have heard of supervisors who read the brief out and then say, 'but I don't personally think that is going to happen'!

All those who carry out such briefings must be trained to understand and use the brief properly, and to field any questions and comments that might arise. Provided briefings are carried out regularly and honestly, they can help to build trust. This involves real effort to achieve clarity and to answer questions promptly and honestly. Sometimes the supervisor or team leader will not have the information to answer legitimate queries. She must not attempt an answer on the spot, but feel free to refer the question back to more senior management – and expect a prompt reply.

The frequency of briefing group meetings is a matter of judgement. Monthly is common, but in a fast-changing situation, weekly briefings might be required. You must be clear about one thing. Although preparing briefing material may seem a chore, it must be done regularly and consistently, but not in a boring manner. It may be useful to pass the responsibility for collating the briefing around to different people from time to time. Urge each collator to vary the style and content. In some organizations, briefs are prepared after the regular round of management meetings. The advantage of this is that any decisions that have been made about machinery, maintenance, scheduling, holidays, covering for absences and so on can be included in an up-to-the-minute brief.

'Preparing briefing material may seem a chore, but it must be done regularly and consistently. Pass the duty around.'

Briefing groups are typically for 3 to 20 or so people. It is rare for regular monthly or weekly briefings to be given to larger groups. In most organizations, the logistics of holding large, frequent meetings is not practicable. However, some organizations may find that an annual meeting involving larger numbers will prove helpful. Otherwise, it is wise to avoid large meetings unless there has been very careful preparation and a clear purpose.

Representational groups

The methods above can be used to reach every individual. There may be occasions, however, when it is more convenient to convey information through representational groups, such as departmental committees, site committees, safety committees or works councils. Typically these committees will consist of elected representatives, management and sometimes one or more experts, for example the personnel officer or the safety officer. As it is usual for these committees to be consulted rather than just informed, they will be described in more detail in Chapter 9.

Special events

There are occasions when it is essential for large numbers of people to receive the same information at precisely the same time. If a decision has been made to shut down a whole factory or office complex at short notice, people must be told quickly before the rumours start. If the company has been taken over, employees must be told about the implications for their unit and their future prospects. The news may not be bad. The firm may wish to announce a success, a new pay deal or a new share distribution to employees (see also Chapter 9 where generating feedback in large meetings is described).

The most effective way to convey such information is to call people together in a large room. If necessary, several large meetings (for example one at each site) can be held at precisely the same time. At each of these meetings, a senior person must deliver the message and deal with questions. The message may mean considerable uncertainty for individuals. It may be desirable to offer individuals the opportunity to see someone for advice or counselling. The arrangements will need to be put in place quickly. Needless to say, the message must be the same in every meeting, and the briefing notes must cover all foreseeable questions. In an organization seeking empowerment, it is vital to be honest, even in difficult times. Most people find uncertainty more difficult to handle than bad news.

'Most people find uncertainty more difficult to handle than bad news.'

There are also rare situations where the emphasis is on everyone receiving the same information, but where the timing is less critical. The classic case is where management is seeking the cooperation of the workforce, but where the intentions or the precise details of new pay and working conditions on offer have become obscured as a result of a breakdown in communications. In these special circumstances, the management may wish to ensure that its message is conveyed to every employee.

Two methods are commonly used. One is to send a letter to every individual at his or her home. The other method is to take out an advertisement in one or more newspapers. The problem with the newspaper solution is that it is difficult to ensure that every employee is covered, and it alerts the whole community to the firm's problems. Once an organization has embraced empowerment concepts, management should find no need to resort to such methods.

Person-to-person responsibilities

In the previous sections, we have covered situations where the same message is to be put across to everyone. There is also the question of giving individuals the information they need to function effectively. In the induction and initial training of new employees, it is important to stress the open culture of the organization. This message will be reinforced by involving a variety of people in this process so that the newcomer realizes that this is not mere sophistry, but the way the organization functions.

The individual has a responsibility to take charge of his own development, but should be aided in this by his team leader, supervisor or manager and his colleagues. Every employee also needs to have someone who takes a particular interest in his performance and development. This is particularly valuable when an individual suffers from discrimination due to race, gender or disability. At more senior levels, the immediate manager will adopt this role. At the sharp end, this will be the team leader or supervisor. It must be made clear that in an empowered organization every manager, supervisor and team leader has responsibilities towards the people who report to her. She is not merely responsible for output, productivity and quality.

'The individual has a responsibility to take charge of his own development.'

The 'people' responsibility means making sure that the individual understands what is required and has been properly trained to do all the tasks involved. The individual must have an opportunity to make suggestions about the job and his own personal development. The supervisor or team leader must be prepared to augment that training and provide coaching and counselling to aid development.

The extent to which these processes need to be formalized (for example, in an appraisal system) depends on the organization. Beware of the trap of putting all the procedures and paperwork systems in place without the commitment to make them work. Commitment can be enhanced by involving people in the development of procedures and systems. Commitment from the top, demonstrated by time devoted to coaching and counselling, is crucial.

Work groups and project groups

How do you ensure effective information flow to and from work groups and project groups? And within those groups?

When a team arrives for work, information may be required about a number of matters. Computer systems can provide data about raw materials and work in progress, priorities, the status of equipment and suchlike. Individual items of work will normally be accompanied by the relevant documentation. In a shift work system, the team on the preceding shift may leave messages in written form. However, often a face-to-face handover is preferable. For routine work, data, documents and notes may be all that is required on a regular basis, but, from time to time, this will need to be supplemented by the team briefing referred to above.

The written communications made at shift handover can take several forms. In some organizations, information is passed from shift to shift simply in the form of written notes on paper or specially prepared forms. Problems arise when these notes become mislaid. Some companies use a white board on which team members can write with marker pens any items they wish to draw to the attention of the incoming workers. They can include problems with machines, products or raw materials supply or changes in priorities. The messages can then be readily erased. This system has the advantage that, because the message is constantly changing, it is worth looking at the board at the start of every shift. Furthermore, the board cannot be blown away, as sometimes happens with pieces of paper in a busy factory. The disadvantage is that the information is lost once it has been erased. In most cases, though, this does not matter.

'How do you ensure effective information flow to and from work groups and project groups? And within those groups?'

Notes about machine problems or defective raw materials are worth a more permanent record. If a machine fault recurs, it may be worth while to investigate it. A pattern in information systems or machine failure is more likely to be recognized if proper records are kept. In many manufacturing companies, it has been the practice to have a book by each machine to record such problems. Some companies have incorporated this record into their computer system. Operatives, maintenance fitters and electricians log in their comments on machine behaviour. They can then call up this information before carrying out routine maintenance or repairs. This will focus attention on a possible design fault or weakness in the equipment should they occur.

'All these written systems will fail if the employees do not make the entries or write up the notes.'

All these systems will fail if the employees do not make the computer entries or write up the notes. In many organizations, inadequate communications between shifts and between work groups are a constant headache. The solution is to gain the commitment of the workforce to these communication procedures or, better still, to get them to work out what communication systems are needed to make the organization work effectively. The more people become involved in creating these systems and understand why they are needed and who they will help, the more they will make them work.

Project groups pose a different problem. In an empowered organization, project groups often involve people from the shop floor. They may be drawn from geographically distant parts of the workplace. Meetings must be organized in advance. As with the management of any project, the group must be given a clear brief, timetable, targets and resources. Empowered organizations are essentially open structures where people can talk to each other about their problems, challenges and opportunities. Each project team member can effectively call on the resources of his normal work group to enrich his contribution to solving the problem.

> *'In an empowered organization, information will tend to flow freely to the people who need it, from the people who have it.'*

Thus, although the official channel for communication will be towards the manager who initiated and has overall responsibility for the topic, information is likely to flow all over the place.

The danger with this approach is that half-baked ideas may be put about as firm proposals. Therefore, particular care must be taken to ensure that project team members learn to distinguish clearly between those ideas that are just being tossed around and suggestions that are being seriously considered. There is far less danger of this kind of misinformation developing in an organization characterized by openness, honesty and trust.

Multi-directional flows

In an empowered organization, information will tend to flow freely to the people who need it, from the people who have it. Management needs to observe this flow and use technology, where appropriate, to make it easier. One of the reasons such information fails to flow as it should in some organizations is that people do not know what their colleagues in other departments need. Management may need to initiate some learning activities to facilitate this understanding.

Snapshot *A manufacturing company held some teamwork development workshops for mixed groups of workers. At one workshop, there were fitters, electricians, process workers and packaging machine operators. In discussion, process workers said they did not really understand how the mechanics and electricians saw their roles.*
The facilitator devised a simple group exercise where the participants ▶

> *formed three groups. One group consisted of fitters and electricians, another group of process workers and the third group of packaging machine operators. Each group prepared a brief presentation covering what they saw as their jobs, what they liked about the job, what frustrated them and what made a 'good day' for them.*
>
> *The groups gave their presentations and, as a result, they learned to respect one another more and found practical ways to help each other achieve more productive and satisfying working lives back in the factory.*

Encouraging people with different disciplines or from different departments to meet to discuss specific information needs or arranging temporary transfers of people between departments can sometimes help.

> **Snapshot** *In a government department, a group of technical experts worked alongside a group of administrative staff. Over a period of time, cooperation between the two groups of people deteriorated to the extent that it interfered with the effective working of the department.*
>
> *The Director decided to run some short workshops where the technical and administrative staff worked on some examples of projects that the department was obliged to undertake. They worked step by step through some of the specific tasks that the department had to perform. At each stage, they considered what contribution was made by the technical staff and then what had to be done by the administrative staff.*
>
> *As the examples were discussed, the administrative staff came to recognize the need for the expertise of the technical people and where this was needed in the process. The technical staff became aware of the need for the administrative procedures that they had previously found irksome. They recognized the skill and experience of the administrative staff. As a result of this experience, mutual respect and a sound working relationship was developed, and the effectiveness of the department improved.*

Remember that information is power, and providing people with the information and understanding they need to make sound decisions is one of the keys to empowering the organization.

Progress checklist

Tick the following items when you can honestly answer 'Yes' to the question posed.

Are you confident that you have optimized written communications with the
workforce? ❑

Have you devised an effective briefing system? How will you will feed this system
with information? ❑

Have you trained the people who will deliver the brief? ❑

If you have a major change in prospect, have you planned how you will
communicate this to the workforce? ❑

Do you intend to ensure that every employee has someone responsible for
his progress? ❑

Are you prepared to support a free flow of information within the organization? ❑

Generating feedback

How to generate and handle feedback

- Everyone's opinion matters in an empowered organization.

- Large meetings can be an effective way to introduce ideas and generate discussion – if they are properly managed.

- Workshops to encourage teamwork can accelerate the move towards empowerment.

- Team briefings can prove an effective tool for maintaining a flow of information and ideas between the workforce and management, and between different sections of the workforce.

- Focus groups and brainstorming sessions can be used to thrash out ideas and suggestions.

- Be cautious in your use of surveys and suggestion schemes.

- Generate a free flow of constructive information and ideas.

Snapshot *In 1988, Cadbury Limited made a major investment in a new high-speed, highly automated plant for the manufacture of Creme Eggs. Following this, the management decided that teamwork was the way ahead for the workforce. Workshops were held for the management group and, subsequently, for groups of workers from the plant at Bournville. At the outset of each workshop, the workers were asked to list their concerns and suggestions. For every item in their lists related to their own welfare, there were five or six related to improving the operation.*

The workers included process operatives (who make the eggs), wrapping machine operators, mechanics and electricians. They tackled the assignments they were given with enthusiasm and even designed some assignments for themselves. The training was to facilitate flexibility as well as to enable them to improve the quality of the product.

Management responded in a positive way to concerns expressed in the earlier workshops. As this news reached people due to attend later workshops, the enthusiasm of participants in these events increased. There was a positive buzz of ideas and a determination to improve the operation and the product quality. A shift manager was present throughout each workshop. At the conclusion of each workshop a senior manager attended to hear what the participants thought about their experiences, and to learn about their recommendations for the future.

Everybody came to realize that the managers were learning how to work in teams as well, and that workers needed to help managers to adapt their styles and behaviour. Managers and workers came to recognize that teamwork is not just about achieving the task together, it is about learning together as well. People were keen to share problems and seek solutions. Productivity and quality targets were met.

In an empowered organization, the opinions of every person matter: every individual has a contribution to make to the success of the enterprise. The question is how to persuade people that managers want to hear their views and are prepared to take them into account. Generating feedback from employees can take the form of asking specific questions or for comments on specific topics. In an empowered organization, employees are encouraged to ask questions and make comments and suggestions on any aspect of the firm's activities.

Initially managers seem to fear that this approach will open up a Pandora's box and out will come all the grievances and problems the workforce has been bottling up for decades. If the process of change is managed constructively, there may be some uncomfortable issues raised. These must be heeded and a sensible response given. If there are well-founded complaints – for example, about poor food in the canteen and a leaking roof in the toilets – these must be dealt with promptly. It must be stressed, however, that, in our experience, such issues do not dominate the discussions if the right climate is created.

'Suggestions about the plant and working practices typically flow from a desire for improvement, not sheer bloody-mindedness.'

Once management commitment (outlined in Chapter 6) has been attained, workshops may be held for supervisors, team leaders and people at every level and in every section of the organization. Once the door is opened for people to express their concerns you will find, in most cases, a genuine desire to do the job better, to give a better service and to produce sound, quality products. Comments are made about such items as working methods, the state of the machinery, the quality of raw materials, the bugs in the software and the space in the showroom. These suggestions about the plant and working practices typically flow from a desire for improvement, not sheer bloody-mindedness.

Large meetings

During periods of dramatic changes in an organization, it has become increasingly popular to call large groups of employees together to make announcements about policy. In moving towards empowerment, such meetings can be held, but they should allow for a positive element of feedback as well as merely providing information.

A practical way to achieve this with meetings of up to, say, 100 people, is to divide participants into groups of 8 to 12 people. The groups will work better with a table each. If this is difficult to organize, the people in a group can merely pull their chairs into a circle when they start group discussions. Each group will need a 'facilitator'. The function of the facilitator in this situation is to promote a good discussion, encouraging everybody to contribute their ideas and helping the group to focus on the issues confronting the organization. The facilitator must, at all costs, avoid imposing his ideas on the group, and must not hog the discussion.

Such a meeting normally begins with a senior manager setting out the position of the company, the need for change and a description of the general direction in which management would like to lead the organization. These presentations conclude with a list of the key questions that management would like to put to the employees present and an explanation of the way the consultation exercise will be conducted.

'The policy and direction having been decided, one can then consult on how these ideas are put into practice in each part of the unit.'

Each group is then invited to discuss the points raised and to feed the results of their deliberations back to the whole meeting. To avoid undue repetition, it is possible to allocate one or two issues to each group with a request that they focus on these particular points. As in any consultation exercise, it is important not to ask people to discuss matters that have already been decided. The policy and direction having been decided, one can then consult on how these ideas are put into practice in each part of the unit, what problems are likely to arise, what the obstacles to progress are and what can be done to deal with the problems and overcome the obstacles.

After a suitable period for discussion, the meeting is called to order and a representative of each group, in turn, addresses the meeting. He or she tells the meeting what the three or four key points arising from the group discussion are. The spokesperson for the group may be the facilitator, but it is better for the group to appoint someone else from among their number to act as the reporter. This enables the facilitator to focus on the group process rather than focusing on the topic under discussion and taking notes. It also means that as the group has appointed its own reporter, there is less danger of the message being distorted by the reporter.

After each mini-presentation, the director or senior manager present has an opportunity to respond to the points raised. Remember that, at this stage, honesty, openness and trust must be displayed. It might be painful for management as there might still be secrets that cannot be divulged. However, if there are secrets, say so. This is far better than prevarication or filibustering. It is a good idea to ask the reporter or facilitator from each group to provide a written summary of the key points. Management can then arrange for a response to all of these points, in writing, in due course.

Such meetings can be enriched by asking people to list the concerns they would like to see addressed. If the general direction of change is known before the meeting, concerns can be gathered beforehand. Ask people to write them down and hand them into someone – perhaps in the personnel department or a member of the management of change project team. The ideas, suggestions and concerns can then be collated and included in the briefing for the discussion groups in the mass meeting. As an alternative, each group facilitator can ask their own group to voice any major concerns and then choose one or two topics to include in that group's discussion.

Mass meetings can last a couple of hours. They must be neither rushed nor kept going for too long. Careful planning and 'stage management' is essential. Stage management is used to ensure that the right message is conveyed and that real opportunities for participation are created. Stage management should not be used to stifle comment nor should any attempt be made to deceive people.

'Mass meetings can last a couple of hours. They must be neither rushed nor kept going for too long.'

It is difficult to generate effective feedback in meetings with substantially more than 100 or so participants. In such cases, it is possible to ask for questions and comments from the floor, but this is rarely a satisfactory way to conduct a consultation. Most people will not get a chance to speak:

One is likely to get the most vociferous, but not the most constructive or intelligent, people contributing. The discussion quickly degenerates into 'sound bites' and slick answers rather than considered views. It is easy for opinions to become polarized and for issues to appear to be irresolvable. What is spoken is rarely in any sense typical of the whole group and it is easy to get an unrepresentative picture of people's opinions this way.

Teamwork workshops

Many organizations have found that once the management commitment has been obtained, teamwork workshops form an effective vehicle for training and development. The workshop format provides an opportunity for people to work and to learn together. Workshops can be held for senior managers on their own, senior managers with front-line managers, front-line managers with team leaders, front-line managers with team leaders and team members.

'The workshop format provides an opportunity for people to work and to learn together.'

Although there is much that managers can learn in workshops on their own, there is no substitute for the learning they achieve when they work alongside team leaders and team members. New relationships can be formed. A new level of respect and mutual understanding can be achieved. In organizations that are moving from a strong control and command culture, managers are often amazed to find out how much the people on the shop floor and in the offices care about their customers and the products and services provided to them. They are also surprised to learn how much the workers are able and willing to contribute in terms of their ideas and suggestions for improvement, when management starts to take them seriously.

A format that has been used successfully for workshops with people drawn from different parts of the organization begins with an introduction and explanation by a senior manager. Workshops with 15–18 employees plus up to a couple of managers are ideal. A competent facilitator is essential. Participants are divided into three groups and asked to list their concerns – in the light of the direction indicated by the senior manager. For example, if the senior manager has announced that the organization wants to move towards more teamwork and products of services that are of a higher quality, people may express concern about a number of issues. They may be concerned about their jobs, bonus schemes, shift patterns, the quality of raw materials, the availability of machine tools, the level of maintenance.

The groups will talk for about 20 minutes and then reassemble to hear each other's points. The facilitator can collect these points (for example, using an overhead projector). He will seek to ensure that these points are all understood by everyone – especially the managers present. He will also do his utmost to see that these points are discussed during the workshop or that there is a commitment to deal with them as soon as possible afterwards.

This is followed by some simple exercises where the groups are asked to prepare brief presentations on topics relevant to the change programme. Topics could include how to improve communications, teamwork, shift handovers, product quality, sales performance, product presentation, response to customer demands. Following the groups' discussions, representatives of the groups will present their findings. This part of the workshop is an opportunity for participants to reflect on their teamwork in the groups (often with a simple questionnaire) and to practise giving and receiving praise and constructive criticism. It is wise to break up the session with a suitable film. Groups can then briefly discuss the key themes that were given in the film.

The last task for the groups is to consider what should happen next – in terms of the action they can take, and that management can take, to move the change programme forward. When these ideas are presented, the senior manager who opened the workshop reappears to hear the views expressed and to give a response.

Workshops of this character normally take at least eight hours to work through to a satisfactory conclusion. For people who are not used to this type of work, five hours or so at a time is enough. It is better to split the workshop up into two halves, each of three to five hours. A large room is required so that the groups can move into the corners. An alternative is to use syndicate rooms that are close to a main meeting room.

'For people who are not used to workshop-style events, five hours or so at a time is enough.'

This format ensures:

- that people are interested in the topics – they relate to their everyday experience
- that people gain a picture of the whole enterprise as the team, not just their own working group
- that new relationships are forged between people in different sections and at different levels
- that the insights gained can be applied directly at the workplace.

As successive groups of people attend the workshops a momentum builds up as more and more people understand what the programme is about and what it involves.

Some organizations have tried to empower people by using methods such as outdoor training or generalized team-building exercises to train people in team-work and improve their self-confidence. There can be no doubt that some individuals have benefited from such activities, but we are not convinced that this is a sound strategy for developing an empowered organization.

Team briefings

The use of briefing groups as a vehicle for disseminating information was described in Chapter 8. Here we are concerned with a more active use of briefing groups where there is a deliberate policy of encouraging team members to comment on some of the issues raised by management and to be prepared to raise issues of their own. Such a policy demands more from the managers preparing the brief and those leading the briefing sessions.

The written briefs must now contain, from time to time, items about which the views of employees are sought. The briefs must also contain answers to questions raised by the workforce or responses to suggestions they have made – provided these are of general interest. Responses that are very specific to a team should be dealt with separately. As with the information-only briefs, it is vital to keep feeding the system with new and interesting information.

The team briefing sessions will generally be confined to the team members concerned. But the system can be used flexibly to encourage cooperation between teams, for example, by occasionally holding joint team briefing sessions where all the members of two teams meet together. If this is not practicable, perhaps several representatives from each of two or even three teams could meet together. The function of these joint briefing sessions is to discuss matters that concern people in the two or three teams involved. For example, the three teams that use the same machines on three successive shifts may meet to discuss how best to use the equipment. They might discuss how to improve the handover. Two teams that are in a customer–provider relationship might discuss the services they provide for each other and the information they need to operate effectively.

'Coordination is achieved by people getting together to understand each other's problems and finding a way to help each other to succeed.'

The point is that, in an empowered organization, this type of coordination is not best achieved by managers – or even experts – laying down procedures. Rather, it is achieved by people getting together to understand each other's problems and finding a way to help each other to succeed. Improvements in procedures and methods will come about because people see the need and want to make them work. All too often in the past, inappropriate systems have been introduced that take up a lot of time and fail to deliver the information people need when they need it and in a digestible form.

Focus groups and brainstorming sessions

Focus groups are often used as a way of gaining 'typical' views and opinions. An opportunity for this is presented when there is something to debate, for example, the merits of a new product, or a new policy, or a new procedure.

The procedure is to choose a group of individuals that are typical of the people who will use, buy or benefit from the product, policy or procedure. Then, a chairperson stimulates discussion on the topic and on the key issues to be explored. A focus group is not composed of people who formally 'represent' the group from which they are drawn. They have no mandate to speak on behalf of the group, but this method is a useful way to explore issues and to refine ideas before going public. Focus groups can last for a couple of hours or a couple of days.

A brainstorming session is a very powerful way to address a specific problem. Here, you need to bring together the 'actors', the people who can make decisions. To do the job properly, allow several hours. Make sure that the chairperson or a facilitator takes you through each of the key steps in the brainstorming process. The first step is to clarify the problem and the parameters involved. The participants are invited to rattle out all their ideas. Any suggestions – however wild and improbable – are written up for all to see on a flip chart or an acetate on an overhead projector. Nobody is allowed to question, criticize or even raise an eyebrow at this stage. Once it appears that ideas have dried up, each suggestion is considered in turn and an explanation sought.

'A brainstorming session is a very powerful way to address a specific problem.'

At this stage, any criticism – explicit or implied – is strictly forbidden. The idea is to ensure that everybody really understands the suggestion. All too often, people put their own interpretation on a suggestion and reject it without really listening to what the proposer has said. People sometimes think of more ideas as those listed are explained. These new ideas are added to the list and explored in turn.

Once the participants have understood all the ideas, these are examined once more and their feasibility examined. Now criticism is legitimate and, indeed, necessary. Gradually, participants will start to prioritize the ideas, rejecting some as being clearly impractical. A smaller list of ideas worth exploring emerges. These ideas are then costed and subjected to cost–benefit analysis, when such questions are asked as: is the likely gain worth the projected cost – in terms of people's time and discomfort, as well as in financial terms? Hopefully, participants will come to agree on the ideas that can be taken forward and formulate an action plan. As in many of these participative processes, you must allow sufficient time in order to achieve the best results.

Snapshot *A company was concerned at the high labour turnover in one of its operational units. The Managing Director gathered together the Personnel Manager from head office and the heads of each of the operating units, plus the Personnel Officer from each unit. The teams from all the units were invited so that the situations could be compared. Furthermore, they needed to be there because any proposed changes (for example, in working hours or conditions) in the unit experiencing high labour turnover could have an impact on practices in the other units.*

The employment situation in the areas where the various units were located differed markedly. The high labour turnover was in the unit situated in an affluent area with plentiful employment opportunities ▶

and relatively high levels of pay. Thus, the MD announced that increasing pay rates was not an option in the immediate future. Labour turnover was having an adverse effect on the performance of the unit and means had to be found to bring about improvements.

Once the parameters of the problem had been established, over 30 suggestions arose from the initial brainstorming session. These were then explored each in turn and 18 rejected as being impractical.

After lunch, each of the remaining 12 ideas was examined in more detail and costed. Seven were selected for action. These were mainly concerned with more flexible working hours, the improvement of facilities and upgrading the working environment.

Those who attended the sessions felt that the issues had been thoroughly explored and they were committed to implementing the actions agreed. A measure of improvement resulted over the ensuing months, but the problem was not fully resolved until pay was increased in line with the local labour market.

Surveys and suggestion schemes

The use of surveys in initiating change was discussed in Chapter 6. It is possible to use surveys on a periodic basis to chart the shift in people's opinions. It is also possible to use survey methods to give people an opportunity to contribute their ideas to the development of the organization. The problem with carrying out a written survey in this connection is that if it consists mainly of forced-choice questions, it leaves little room for creative suggestions. On the other hand, if there are too many open questions, the results will be difficult to analyze.

An organization that moves towards empowerment faces a dilemma over suggestion schemes. On the one hand it is a tried and trusted method for encouraging employees to put forward constructive ideas, for which they can be rewarded. On the face of it this seems wholly consistent with the empowerment concept. However, suggestion schemes generally require the individual to think through his idea in some detail and to submit this formally for evaluation. In an empowered organization, individuals are prepared to share their ideas immediately with others and to contribute to the continuous improvement of the operation. It is therefore dysfunctional to continue with a suggestion scheme unless it can be regarded as a vehicle for those with really major money-saving ideas. Mostly, we want the ideas to be out on the table quickly and implemented as soon as practicable.

Dynamic interaction

Meetings, written communications and computer data of one kind or another – all these form the infrastructure of effective communications. But these devices are not enough. The will to communicate and the will to listen and take notice are far more important – that is the culture of the empowered organization. Get this right and the information will flow in all directions in a sensible and constructive manner.

Management must ensure that this kind of dynamic interaction is positively encouraged. The way you achieve it depends on your circumstances. You might consider allowing a few minutes at the beginning of each shift for a handover meeting and equipping each area with a white board. It might be helpful to provide team rooms where people can meet. Project teams can be set up involving people from different sections and levels to look at specific problems and challenges. In many cases, such initiatives will arise from the suggestions of your people. Listen to them.

Progress checklist

Tick the following items when you can honestly answer 'Yes' to the question posed.

Have you decided as a matter of policy to let everybody have a say in the way the business is run? ❑

Have you determined what large meetings you consider useful? Who will organize these? ❑

Do you see a place for teamwork workshops? ❑

Have you a plan to use team briefings for multidirectional communications? ❑

Have you decided what role, if any, you see for focus groups and brainstorming sessions? ❑

Have you considered to what extent ongoing surveys and/or suggestion schemes have a place? ❑

Are you prepared to encourage a dynamic information flow in your organization? ❑

10 Sharing and negotiating

How and when to share decisions

- Learn to delegate with confidence.

- Coaching helps both people concerned.

- Open organizations need 'delegated' communications.

- Joint decisions depend on shared goals.

- Negotiation will be needed in some areas.

- Formal structures can help ongoing communications.

- Committees need feeding and nurturing.

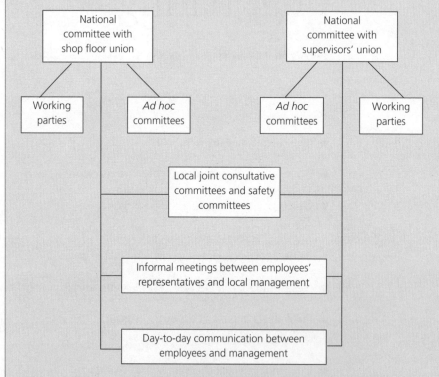

Snapshot *Figure 3 describes the committee structure in a service company that has maintained effective communications with its workforce for many years. In each case, the lines represent two-way communications. The effectiveness of the system has waxed and waned according to the amount of effort made by management to keep it alive.*

Figure 3 A committee structure that helps effective communications

Senior managers are convinced that the flow of information has helped to avoid misunderstanding and maintained the morale of the workforce. Industrial action is almost unknown and effective communication is one of the factors that has helped to maintain this situation.

Sharing the decision-making process is a risky business. Decisions can be shared in two ways:

- they can be delegated
- they can be made jointly.

If there are significant areas where a potential conflict of interests exists, negotiation is necessary.

Delegation

Empowered organizations have fewer layers of management than those with a command and control culture. This means that delegation becomes a necessity. In flatter organizations, managers simply do not have the time to make all the decisions themselves. In many control and command organizations, middle managers become almost like postal sorting offices – messages passing through their hands with very little need for action on their part. In an empowered organization, the pattern of communications becomes far more complicated – communication itself becomes delegated.

> 'A manager can delegate if he believes that the person to whom he has given the authority is likely to make the right decision.'

A manager can delegate if he believes that the person to whom he has given the authority is likely to make the right decision. Decisions vary in their importance, and rarely will a manager delegate the most crucial decisions. However, in a typical workplace there are numerous day-to-day decisions that can be made by people at the sharp end.

It is worth while thinking through some of the criteria one might use to delegate decisions. It is rare to find the perfect boss who makes no poor decisions. Thus, in reality, it is often too much to expect that every delegated decision will be the best. However, provided the individual is not likely to make more poor decisions than his boss, delegation becomes an option.

Three key factors influence behaviour, including decision-making behaviour. These three key factors are the:

- individual's ability
- circumstances in which the decision is made
- individual's motivation at the time.

Individuals cannot be expected to make sound decisions if they have not learned how to gather relevant information, 'read the signs', evaluate the data, consider alternative options and choose the optimum actions from all the other possibilities. These skills can be taught, to an extent, off the job, but, in the workplace, the best method is often for one individual to 'coach' another, working through the decisions that actually have to be made. The 'coach' has to learn coaching skills. If the coach is the manager, this has the added advantage of helping the manager to gain confidence in her subordinate.

In an empowered organization, coaching can work between peer and peer and between subordinate and boss. Often the worker on the front line has a lot of knowledge and skills relating to the job, equipment, customers, materials and suchlike, that he can pass on to the boss. In organizations that seek empowerment, a lot of learning has to take place across departmental boundaries. People need to understand each other's jobs, the demands on them, how they can help each other. Much of this learning can be achieved by people coaching each other at all levels. And coaching can go in both directions at once. Peter helps Jane with one problem, while Jane helps Peter with another. This is sometimes called co-coaching. Often this activity is simply two people having a chat about the job.

> 'Team spirit must start at the top, with no dysfunctional rivalries between departmental heads.'

As indicated in Chapter 3, having the ability to make the right decision is not enough. People must have the right conditions, the right information at the right time and a clear understanding of their responsibilities and the authority they can wield. People at the sharp end cannot be expected to make sound decisions if they are starved of information about the priorities of the business and the cost implications of alternative actions. They need this in addition to detailed data about the current products and services and the tasks they need to perform.

Encouraging every individual to be motivated to work for the benefit of the organization is a more elusive achievement. Conflicts of interest arise, for example, when one must decide to lend another team some people because their need is greater than yours. Tackling job A before job B may help the next section in the line, but it will mean that your own productivity will decline. It would suit your operation better to complete work on B. That is a tough choice – unless you are motivated to work in the best interests of the firm rather than yourself. It also assumes that your reward system (Chapter 4) is not structured such that you are penalized for such helpful behaviour.

This level of motivation is achieved only by viewing the whole enterprise as the team, not just your local work group. Such team spirit must start at the top, with no dysfunctional rivalries between departments or departmental heads. It must be constantly reinforced.

The final piece in the jigsaw is the need for the person with the authority to gain confidence in the people to whom that authority is to be delegated. It is not enough that the people are able, have the data and are motivated, the boss must believe it. Otherwise she will never let go. She will always be chasing up the decisions, shadowing the subordinate, asking unnecessary questions simply to be assured that all is well.

Snapshot *The boss of a public-sector body was worried about a new programme where a number of visits and assessments had to be made by a given date. As the date approached, he would rush early to the office on each Monday morning and get the latest figures on the programme. When the departmental head appeared, he would be confronted with the data and asked to explain the results.*

As a matter of fact, the whole operation had been carefully planned, with contingency time built into the programme. The departmental head had delegated the detail to his section heads. He simply did not have the information to rebut the office figures. The office figures were always behind the action in the field as it took time for individual advisers to check in with their results. The departmental head did not waste the time of his section heads by asking for more information.

Looking at the data carefully it was easy to see that the programme was on course. It was completed on time and there were only 5 complaints out of 2,500 assessments. All of the complaints were resolved in house, without reference to external arbitration.

The criteria for delegation can thus be summarized in a seven-point plan:

1 choose the potential areas of delegation
2 ensure that people acquire the skills they need to make sound decisions; encourage co-coaching
3 provide the right conditions for decisions to be made
4 create a common purpose that people can share and ensure that they understand this clearly
5 create and maintain a culture that motivates people to behave in support of the common purpose

6 delegate decisions progressively, monitoring results and providing coaching support

7 learn to trust the people to whom you delegate.

Delegation of communications

Delays in communications occur frequently within the command and control structures because messages are routed through the hierarchy. An operative wants a machine fault rectified. He tells the supervisor. The supervisor tells the production manager who informs the maintenance manager who tells the maintenance supervisor who then has to find a fitter to attend to the machine. In the meantime, the operative has finished her shift and nobody knows what is wrong with the machine.

In empowered organizations, the operative goes straight to the fitter. The fitters know what the priorities are and can make the decision to attend to the machine or not there and then. If the problem the fitter is currently dealing with has a higher priority, both the fitter and the operative will appreciate that. If the operative's problem is also urgent, the fitter may turn to a colleague within his team for help or somebody in another team. In a command and control culture, such behaviour would end in chaos, but in an empowered organization it is an everyday occurrence.

As we have stressed before, this illustrates the key points about delegation and teamwork. The organization is the team so that the fitter, the operative and anybody else drawn into the situation is concerned to achieve organizational goals, not just solve the immediate problem. You can allow people to communicate freely with each other if they share the goals of the organization, understand the current priorities, appreciate the problems of their colleagues and have access to appropriate information.

Joint decisions

Joint decisions are made when people meet together to discuss matters where they must all act in concert, often exercising a measure of give and take. Such decisions are possible when their view of the shared goal takes precedence over their personal or team interest. The allocation of existing resources is often a key issue. People tend to be protective of any resources they possess and will not readily surrender them to another section. This problem is exacerbated if the individual work groups are forged into strong teams at the expense of viewing the whole firm as the team.

> **Snapshot** *The managers of a warehouse were eager to encourage an empowered teamwork culture. Before the introduction of the teamwork culture there were shift supervisors, not team leaders. Shift supervisors typically competed for staff and could not agree such reallocations. These had to be imposed by the manager. The decision often left some disgruntled supervisors in its wake. This was a function of the culture, not the individuals concerned.*
>
> *To initiate teamwork, employees responsible for handling cartons of products were reorganized into groups and trained in teamwork. Each team had a team leader who was a hands-on working member of the team. At the beginning of each shift, these team leaders met together to review the workload in relation to the number of people available. They then agreed on any reallocation of staff from one team to another. Partway through the shift the team leaders met together to review progress and, if necessary, reallocate staff.*

If it is not possible to wean people off this preoccupation with parochial concerns, then the matter must be negotiated or a solution imposed by a higher authority – the boss of the people concerned. The more this is necessary, the further away will the team be from an empowerment culture. The essence of joint decision making is the sharing of goals, so the structures and the procedures must reflect this concern. For *ad hoc* decisions, the project group and the problem-solving workshop are effective methods.

The project group can be used when it is possible to identify a problem where the solution depends on cooperation between several individuals or groups. The project team will consist of a leader and representatives of the individuals concerned. The team may need access to expert help and, in some cases, the expert will become a member of the team. At the outset, the project team needs a clear brief and target dates. At least one member of the team should be thoroughly conversant with problem-solving and project management methods. Encourage project team members to consult widely with their colleagues.

In a control and command culture, there is a tendency to keep all the deliberations somewhat secret so that people do not run off with half-baked ideas and get upset. In an organization that values honesty and trust, such secrecy is out of place. People must learn the difference between ideas being floated and firm proposals.

The problem-solving workshop is particularly valuable if the problem is charged with emotion or tainted with misunderstanding. Such overtones tend to arise as a result of ignorance – of the other group's situation, opinions or actions. In a problem-solving workshop, such differences of view diminish as the focus is then on the problem and its solution. The focus is no longer on what people think about each other. As people start to consider what they can do together to improve the situation, a mood of cooperation and mutual support can be engendered.

'Senior managers must exhibit interest in problem-solving activities. If the problem is not of concern to management, why tackle it?'

The interest of senior management in these problem-solving activities must be evident. Indeed, if the problem is not a concern to management, why tackle it? Senior managers should look in on meetings, enquire about progress and give positive praise and encouragement, whilst leaving the group to get on with the job. Deserved praise is one of the key lubricating mechanisms in any human endeavour. Another factor is constructive criticism. The more difficult and important the problem, the more people need encouragement and support.

Negotiation and effort bargains

Negotiation is necessary when one person or group of people perceive that they will lose out when a decision is to the advantage of another individual or group. The question of financial rewards is probably the commonest example. More rewards for the workers means higher costs to the company and, perhaps, lower profits for the investors. The equation is not that simple, but that is how it is often perceived and it is the question of perception that is all important here. People's behaviour is based on how they see things, not necessarily on how things actually are.

In an empowered organization, where one or more trade unions are recognized for bargaining purposes, one would expect to see an honest and open discussion about what the company can afford and what the workforce is entitled to receive. In some countries, the culture that the managers and workforce of the organization work together to maximize profitability and success is well established, and they only then see about dividing up the cake. It is in the shared interests of both the company and the workforce to achieve prosperity and survival. However, the division of the financial gains is a proper matter for negotiation.

If there are two or more interest groups on the employees' side, then the allocation of rewards across these groups is a sensitive matter, particularly when the rewards systems are changed to encourage empowerment. Organizations that seek empowerment bring all the parties together at a 'single table', rather than negotiate with the trade unions one by one as arrangements that suit production operatives may not suit fitters and electricians or office staff.

However, the concept goes beyond negotiations about rewards. It can occur when one section in the organization wants changes to be made to operational procedures and these impact on another section. Often many such difficulties can be resolved by relying on a shared interest in achieving better results. A useful method is to set up a small project team to investigate the problem, discuss alternatives with the people involved and suggest the way ahead. There may still be some residual areas of disagreement when these processes have been exhausted. Then the problem moves into the area of give and take.

'If the culture is supportive, effort bargains will solve many frictional problems.'

Some of the items involved will be tangible or procedural – the use of equipment or space, the timing or sequence of some procedures, the collection of data in certain ways. They may require changes in shift patterns, working times, working at weekends and similar issues. These are sensitive matters.

In the deals that are struck, a useful concept is the 'effort bargain'. This is where there may be no exchange of tangible resources, but merely a commitment to behave differently in the way people help each other. Put simply an 'effort bargain' is an agreement that if one party behaves in certain ways, the other will respond in return – 'I will do this if you will do that.' If the culture is supportive, this attitude and behaviour will solve many of the frictional problems that hinder effective cooperation.

There are three essential steps in the negotiating process:

- preparation
- discussion
- implementation.

In an empowered organization, all three processes are enriched by the culture of honesty, openness and trust. Instead of posturing and playing games, people can get on with the business of teasing out the issues, establishing the facts and working out a solution. Each 'side' should not be following a 'we win, you lose strategy', but seeking a win–win outcome, where everyone feels that a fair deal has been struck.

In preparing for negotiation each side will sit down and review:

- the current situation, as seen by your side
- how you think the other side sees the situation
- the key outcomes you desire from the negotiation
- what you think the other side wants from the negotiation.

As you consider outcomes, you may be able to put alongside each point the minimum you require as well as your preferred solution. Similarly, you may be able to identify these factors for each of the points you expect the other side to raise. In an open organization, there should be few surprises when the two sides meet. Be prepared to consider requirements put to you by the other side that have no bearing on the matter under discussion. When you want something, this provides an opportunity for the other side to voice a request.

In conducting the discussions, each side will outline its position and its requirements (not 'demands'). Each of the desired outcomes can be examined in turn and, with give and take on both sides, a solution should be possible that pleases all concerned. This does not imply that everybody gets what they want on every point. You can yield somewhat on some points and gain on others provided the overall package is satisfactory. This is one of the reasons it is necessary to ensure that the negotiations are not about a single issue, that is a go or no go situation. Break the problem down into constituent parts.

The two factors that normally disrupt negotiations are when one side makes an unreasonable, or an unexpected demand. An unexpected demand means that someone has not done his homework – communications have broken down somewhere along the line. When this occurs it is useful for the two sides to retire to separate rooms so that they can prepare again, taking this new factor into account. An unreasonable demand means that trust has broken down. This is because an unreasonable demand implies that one side believes that the other can deliver on the demand without damage. If that is not so, then the side making the demand does not believe it: they do not trust the other side.

Assuming that a satisfactory deal can be struck, you must broadcast the results so that everybody knows just what has been agreed. Confirm it in writing quickly to stem any misunderstanding. This is entirely consistent with an open culture. If you are negotiating on behalf of a particular group of people, make sure they are told of any developments quickly. Make sure that they are informed before news gets back to them via the rumour machine or, worse still, the local paper!

You must be meticulous in the implementation of the deal. It is vital to keep building trust by being true to your word.

Formal structures

If there is a need for ongoing consultation, joint decisions and negotiations it is wise to set up structures for this purpose. If your organization recognizes one or more trade unions, you will need to consider how to involve representatives in the structures that are established. In an organization working towards empowerment, you can take the opportunity to consult your employees about the kind of structures they would favour.

Although the trade unions will normally be your main communications channel concerning employment matters, you must feel free to communicate directly with the workforce about other matters. If a trade union behaves in an irresponsible manner, you may need to contact the workforce directly about employment issues, but this should not be necessary. If you are working for an empowered organization, you will wish to encourage cordial and constructive relationships with the recognized trade union(s).

If you have not recognized any trade union, you will need to consider carefully how the workforce can elect representatives to serve on the committees you establish. You must take steps to ensure that the election system is fair and not influenced by management.

'Whatever structures are established, they need to be fed and nurtured.'

The basic vehicle for information and consultation on general matters may well be the briefing groups. They are not 'representative' in an elected sense, but these structures can be used to convey information quickly and often to gain a preliminary response to new ideas and proposals. You will need to consider the needs of different sites and also how you can effectively include shift workers who are still working.

Many organizations have set up departmental, site and national committees or works councils to provide opportunities for consultation, and sometimes for joint decision making and negotiating. Health and safety issues constitute a particular concern, and it is common for committees to be established to discuss such matters.

The structure you establish will depend on the size, complexity and geography of your organization and the number of people employed. Typically, the meetings are chaired by a manager at an appropriate level, with equal numbers of management and employee representatives. The agenda would be agreed by both sides and minutes taken, agreed and circulated. The minutes may be distributed more widely or posted on noticeboards. Minutes so posted are rarely read by individual employees. It is better to summarize the main points in a newsletter (see Chapter 8) where the information can be conveyed in an attractive fashion.

Whatever structures are established, they need to be fed and nurtured. There can be few things worse than sitting through a committee going through the motions, with nothing better to discuss than the minutes of the last meeting. Make sure that there are interesting topics and that these committees are informed about developments in the company.

The nature of the agenda and the information provided will depend on the coverage of the committee. Local committees need some of the same information as the national committees, but they also want to know about local issues that affect their department or site. In an empowered organization, these committees should be but the tip of an iceberg of effective communications.

Progress checklist

Tick the following items when you can honestly answer 'Yes' to the question posed.

Can you recognize examples of when delegation, joint decision making and
negotiations are appropriate? ❑

Do you agree with the criteria for effective delegation in an empowered
organization? ❑

Can you apply these criteria in your organization? ❑

Have you decided to encourage coaching and co-coaching? ❑

Can you see opportunities for joint decision making in your organization? ❑

Do you have an effective strategy for negotiations? ❑

Are your people trained in negotiation procedures? ❑

Are you satisfied with the formal consultation structures in your organization? ❑

Do you have a system for feeding and nurturing committees? ❑

11

Managing business relationships

Managing the interfaces with stakeholders

- Organizations exist to satisfy needs.

- Many shareholders are interested in ethical matters.

- Service to the customer is enhanced if employees are empowered.

- You need the commitment of employees and subcontracted workers who are not in full-time, permanent contracts.

- Consider the position of contract staff working regularly alongside your people.

- Your organization's interaction with the local community can prove a positive factor in your success.

> **Snapshot** *Marks & Spencer, a retail company formed in 1884, is regarded as one of the most spectacular corporate successes in the UK. It is widely recognized as being one of the best-managed companies in the world. The company has embraced a set of principles. M&S aims to offer to its customers a selective range of high-quality, well-designed and attractive merchandise at reasonable prices under the brand of St Michael.*
>
> *It works with its suppliers to encourage the use the most modern and efficient production techniques and to ensure the highest standards of quality control. It fosters good human relations with customers, suppliers and staff, and in the communities where it operates. The company provides friendly, helpful service and shopping comfort and convenience to customers.*
>
> *Improvements in the business are achieved by means of simplifying operational procedures. The success of M&S is attributed to the fact that all levels of staff are encouraged to embrace these principles and to apply them in their day-to-day work. The company invests heavily in good human relations. This long-term investment is not susceptible to conventional cost–benefit analysis, but those who have led M&S over the years have been convinced that without this investment in its own staff, the company would not achieve the level of success it enjoys.*
>
> *M&S does not have a financial stake in its suppliers, but it has, over the years, invested heavily in terms of technical support and management advice. In dealing with suppliers, M&S staff encourage them to adopt an outlook and operating philosophy close to their own. This had led to a close interdependence between M&S and its suppliers and a series of long-term relationships.*

Organizations exist to satisfy needs. A commercial organization has owners, shareholders who expect a return on their investment. Public bodies have owners too, the tax-paying public. They are represented by the political masters who expect that the organizations will fulfil the functions assigned to them in a competent, cost-effective manner.

Organizations have customers or clients, people and other organizations served by the firm or the public body. Organizations also have employees who give their labour and expertise – and expect a fair reward in return. Employees also hope for some measure of job security, but this is becoming a rare commodity.

These three groups, owners, customers and employees, may be considered as the primary stakeholders in an enterprise. There is a requirement to maintain a balance in meeting the needs of the primary stakeholders if the business or public service is to survive and prosper. There are also suppliers, lenders and the public at large to take into account. The public interest is protected by the various regulatory authorities, for example, those responsible for taxation, social services, health and safety and the environment.

'Organizations exist to satisfy needs.'

Relationships with these various stakeholders take on a particular significance for companies that aspire to empowerment. The employment contract now takes many forms. The shareholders may be concerned with issues other than pure monetary gain. Suppliers may not be operating at arm's length but be intimately associated with the business, impacting directly on the way the organization works and the way it is perceived by others. In many types of business, vertical integration is the only way to secure quality and competitive advantage.

Shareholders' concerns

One of the values that underpins empowerment is that people matter, and everybody counts. Shareholders are taking an increasing interest in the way organizations deal with ethical issues. The Churches, charities, local authority pension funds and ethical investors are increasingly concerned about ethical, social and environmental values. These investors exert pressure on the ways in which companies behave.

Thus, the way organizations treat their employees, the impact they have on the environment and their influence in social and health matters can be taken into account by investors. Issues ranging from the spillage of oil and the manufacture of weapons of torture to the effect of promoting milk substitutes on breastfeeding and the nutrition of infants can have an effect on investment decisions.

It is therefore worthwhile considering making public the moves the organization is making towards empowerment in the annual report to shareholders, mentioning this as part of the statement on relations with employees. This statement is in addition to the fact that empowerment is undertaken to improve the profitability of the company. Particular actions taken by the company can also be publicized in the media to inform shareholders and the public at large of the way the company is developing.

The way in which many public-sector bodies now deal with the public demonstrates a shift in culture. Individual employees have more responsibility and flexibility. They must, of course, operate within the policies prescribed, but this does not prevent them from being helpful to the public and considerate in the way they do their jobs.

Customer focus

The most profound impact of empowerment is on the customers. When empowerment becomes a reality for staff who deal with customers, their whole approach changes. Unempowered individuals stick closely to the company's prepared text. They adhere steadfastly to the prescribed procedures. Any request that is out of the ordinary in any way has to be referred to senior people for decisions and action. Empowered employees, however, will be sensitive to customer needs and aware of what the company can do to meet those needs – or is not able to do. They will use the resources of the organization to meet customer demands, making decisions (within reasonable limits) without referring to senior people all the time. If the company cannot meet a customer's needs, but another organization can, they will refer the customer on to another source of supply. We have all had the experience of going into a shop where the assistant could not supply the goods we want and referred us to another shop down the road. We come out of the first shop determined to go back again because we feel warmly disposed to the assistant who helped us. The shop lost a sale, but probably gained a future customer.

'Empowered employees will be sensitive to customers' needs.'

Empowerment at the customer interface implies that the individuals concerned have the authority to use their discretion. It also implies that they have the knowledge and ability to make sensible decisions. It assumes that they are committed to the best interests of the organization. Employees at the customer interface need support from others within the organization.

But the effect of empowerment is not just felt at the customer interface. Empowered employees committed to the organization's goals will exert themselves to ensure that the quality, reliability and delivery of goods and services meet customers' requirements. Such employees will know about their customers, their needs and their circumstances. They will take the trouble to draw these to the attention of other people in the organization so that changes can be made for the benefit of the customers – and for the company as well.

If this area is of particular concern to your organization, then moves towards empowerment should be coordinated with either customer focus programmes or quality improvement initiatives (that is using the international standard for quality management ISO 9000) or both.

Typically, customer care programmes seek to take concern for the customer beyond barely meeting the immediate needs expressed by that customer. The aim is to 'delight' the customer by ensuring that his or her needs are properly understood and met, right first time. A successful customer care programme will not only help to secure existing customers and attract more, it will also increase job satisfaction within the organization. Action by individuals at the sharp end must be backed up by a programme involving senior management commitment, exploring customer needs and developing service standards. It involves attending to all contacts with the customer, including the literature provided, contact on the telephone, ordering, order processing and invoicing procedures, delivery people and after-sales care. The company recruitment and training processes must ensure that people have the skills and attitudes required for this caring process.

Snapshot *A man with a large garden situated on a steep hill was interested in purchasing a garden tractor-mower. He telephoned three companies. One sent him a leaflet about their tractors and another sent him a leaflet about power generators! The third company's telephonist referred him to a technical specialist. The specialist asked him about what he wanted the tractor for, how steep the hill was, how large the area of grass to be cut was and what other uses he envisaged for the machine. Having ascertained that the basic 8 horse power model would not do the job, the technical expert arranged for a dealer to visit the customer with a 12 horse power machine. This, he said, would be able to complete the tasks he required, and would climb the hill with full grass-bags or towing a trailer of hedge clippings or paving slabs.*

The man bought the 12 horse power machine and the relevant accessories. The equipment is still giving sound service ten years later.

Employees and 'portfolio people'

You may remember that the reward system as it applies to employees was discussed in Chapter 4. Over the years, the nature of the labour market changes. Full-time employment with the same employer from the age of 16 to 65, followed by retirement, is no longer the norm. Some workers are not employed by the organization at all. They have a contract to provide services, not a contract of service.

People have been hired as individual subcontractors in the building industry for decades, but this practice is now widespread in many other sectors. Many people now work part-time for more than one employer. They are 'portfolio people' who may offer different services to different people, and who value some free time to follow their own interests. These interests may include looking after their children, mowing the lawn, playing golf or helping the local community. Independent consultants and freelance writers and photographers have operated in this way for decades, but the concept has become more widely adopted – sometimes out of necessity rather than choice.

' "Portfolio people" may offer different services to different people, and value some free time to follow their own interests.'

These people may work closely alongside the full-time employees of your organization. They may well like the open, honest and trusting atmosphere of an empowered organization, but do they have the skills required to work effectively in such a culture? Are they prepared to accept responsibility for their actions and work effectively in a team? It may be necessary to consider an induction programme for such people to help them to acclimatize to working in your organization.

In the case of part-time and fixed-term contract staff, this can be incorporated into the normal induction and initial training programme. Temporary staff may pose a particular problem. If people are pulled in to help out rarely and only to deal with emergencies, for example, to cover for people unexpectedly taken ill, then there may be little to be gained by a special training programme. You may well find that each time you approach the agency, you get a different person.

Some organizations, however, use temporary staff regularly on a larger scale. For example, some organizations employ temporary staff to cover the seasonal peaks in the demand for labour. Many companies in this position seek to train a group of people associated with a particular agency to form a pool of trained labour from which they can draw as required. The training is in the essential skills required for the seasonal tasks to be performed. In an empowered organization, consideration should be given to extending this training to cover the skills of working in this culture.

Suppliers and in-house contractors

Your staff may work cheek by jowl alongside staff from suppliers. Their own ability to perform is undoubtedly affected by the performance of those who supply your organization with goods and services. After all, it is difficult to make good cable out of poor raw materials. It is hard to sell good food if the farmer or the food manufacturer fails to maintain high standards. Good food is soon ruined if the transportation and storage are inadequate. It is difficult to maintain timely pharmaceutical supplies to the chemist shops if your computer system, once installed, does not live up to the supplier's promises. You cannot make decent tin cans if the tinplate is defective. And so it goes on.

For this reason, many firms now work very closely with their suppliers. Instead of simply buying on price and promised delivery dates from a range of suppliers, firms are selecting a limited number of suppliers. They then work with them to determine and specify just what goods and services they require. Their staff work together to see that these criteria are met. They visit each other's premises, make suggestions on how to improve and support each other. They mount joint project teams to tackle shared problems.

'When the contractor's staff are working alongside your own employees, there is scope for cultural osmosis to occur.'

Such intimate working relationships need careful management as there will inevitably be a growing together of the cultures of these organizations. You want to be sure that your suppliers grow towards empowerment, and that your staff do not regress.

Subcontractors who work on your premises present a particular problem. Many companies now focus management attention on core activities, subcontracting out activities that may be essential but are not central to the firm's survival. The contracted-out activities commonly include security, catering and cleaning. They may include accounting, information mail-shots and billing. Some firms also contract out such activities as safety audits, energy audits or environmental impact studies.

When the contractor's staff are working daily alongside your own employees, there is scope for cultural osmosis to occur. You will again need to encourage your contractors to adopt an open, honest and trusting approach in their dealings with their own employees.

Community concerns

The openness, honesty and trust culture that develops in an empowered organization often spills out into the community. Employees can become involved in community improvement projects of different kinds. If the company is able to support this activity in a modest way, there can be reciprocal benefits. Many organizations have found it helpful to second selected staff to voluntary organizations or simply give them some time off to help with a local community action project. This kind of activity can be an excellent way of helping the seconded individual to develop talents and abilities beyond what is possible within the company or public body.

Snapshot *A young executive from a bank was seconded to help a local youth training project in South London.*

In one of the training sessions, the group was discussing managing money. One trainee thought that the executive was talking through his hat. She said to the young manager, 'How much did those shoes cost that you are wearing?' When the manager replied, the trainee said 'Do you realize that that is more money than we get to live on for a fortnight?' The executive was speechless. He had never really thought about that before. It was a lesson he would never forget, and it made him more socially aware and more sensitive to the plight of other people.

If your organization is a substantial employer operating within a multi-ethnic community, you may wish to pay particular attention to equal opportunity initiatives. For example, you may seek to ensure that the various groups are, as far as possible, properly represented within your workforce. Your equal opportunity policy should apply to promotion decisions within your organization, as well as to recruitment activities.

Progress checklist

Tick the following items when you can honestly answer 'Yes' to the question posed.

Do you intend to inform shareholders of your aim to become an empowered
organization? ❑

Will you ensure that empowerment delivers better quality service to your
customers? ❑

Have you considered the benefits of a customer care programme? ❑

Will you take steps to ensure that all the people working for you – including those
working on a part-time or non-permanent basis – will be helped to work in an
empowered culture? ❑

Will you seek to encourage empowerment in the organizations that work closely
with you? ❑

Have you considered how empowerment relates to your impact on
the community? ❑

PART III

Learning and empowerment

12

Learning and development

An overview of ways of helping people to learn

- Learning is fundamental to empowerment and you will need a good grasp of the methods employed.

- Distinguish between planned learning and the dynamic learning required in empowered organizations.

- Consider the essential differences between coaching, counselling and mentoring.

- Ensure that the appraisal process is seen as a forward looking opportunity to improve the operation.

Snapshot *Over the years, a family business that started with one modest guest house has expanded to encompass four substantial hotels in the South West of England. However, the company, Torquay Leisure Hotels experienced a serious fall in profitability in the late 1980s. Customer satisfaction was falling and it became clear that the tight, central control and authoritarian management style that had worked in a single, small guest house was not an option for the future. There was poor communication within the company, limited teamwork and a lack of corporate direction.*

After investigating the problem, the directors decided that there was a need to plan for the future and to focus on customer care. They recognized the need for a new management style and a new culture within the organization.

Six senior managers undertook teamwork training. Other managers received training in operational management. All managers and supervisors were trained to train others and to support training for vocational certificates. Staff were trained in customer care, health, safety and hygiene, and in sales methods. During this extensive training programme, projects were initiated to deal with specific problems and opportunities for improvement. These projects also enhanced the skills of those who worked on them.

What were the results? There was a dramatic improvement in customer satisfaction. The company continued to link its training and development activities with its business plans and has gained the UK 'Investors in People' award. The company has regained, and, indeed, exceeded, its earlier profitability levels.

It is important for those who lead the process of empowerment to understand the elements of learning and development. This will enable them to guide those responsible for particular parts of the action.

One of the basic planks of empowerment is helping people to learn all they can about the organization, the job they are doing and how it all fits together. In some organizations, this encouragement to learn is not limited to the jobs and tasks within the company. Some senior people take the view that once an organization starts to unleash the intellectual power of its employees, the desire to learn should not be curbed. It is important for those who lead the process of empowerment to understand the elements of learning and how this fits into the process.

Learning by means of formal training and education

Over the years, the distinctions between training and education have become blurred. 'Training' is usually associated with helping someone to acquire the knowledge, skills and attitudes necessary to perform a task or job. There are many skills that can be acquired with the help of an instructor. She will typically demonstrate the task to be performed, carefully pointing out the key points of the operation and, in particular, any health or safety problems associated with the activity. Then, the trainee will be given an opportunity to attempt the task, under supervision, and be given feedback on his performance and guidance on how to improve. There follows a period of practice, during which, hopefully, the trainee will develop speed and precision in carrying out the task.

'Many skills can be acquired with the help of an instructor.'

Many of the tasks performed in industry, commerce and the public sector are amenable to this mode of training. It may be used to train an individual to operate a machine in a factory, to issue boarding cards at an airport, to serve a meal in a restaurant or to open an official file. Often it is advisable to analyze the tasks and to highlight key points. The instructor may be a fellow worker, a team leader or a supervisor. It is essential to ensure that the individual helping the learner has been trained to instruct. Many organizations also keep a record of each instructor and the task he is trained to perform.

Education is a broader concept. Education includes training to perform the skills of everyday living (for example, reading, writing, doing sums, getting along with people). Much of what happens in our schools is helping to prepare people for specific areas of employment and careers. The French word 'formation' describes the total process of learning, including education, training and life's experiences. In the 'formation' of a young person, this includes what happens at school, but it also includes what happens at home, in the youth club and in the community. All these forces shape our knowledge, skills, attitudes, beliefs and values.

This French word 'formation' has been imported into the English language as we have no equivalent. The idea is important in an organizational context. It reminds us that, besides what we teach in the training centre and instruct on the job, many other influences are at work, shaping the way people develop and the way they perceive the world of work. People learn by observing others, their peers, their managers and people they respect.

Forward-looking companies make extensive use of appropriate educational resources in helping their people to develop, and many assist their workers to obtain educational and vocational qualifications relevant to their work. Opportunities for adults to obtain a wide range of recognized educational and vocational qualifications exist in many countries, including the United Kingdom, France, Germany and the United States.

The extent to which organizations provide financial support and time off for study varies considerably. Some organizations share the cost of tuition with the employee. They consider that the company contribution is an encouragement to the individual and that the employee's share in the expenses helps to ensure commitment.

Learning at work

Learning is broader than education and training. In helping people to learn it is important to distinguish between different types of learning. For example, knowledge is easier to acquire than a skill, but knowledge is more easily lost than a skill once it has been acquired. Knowledge can fall into the recesses of the mind and not be readily recalled after some time has elapsed. If it is essential to retain some knowledge, then constant revision is necessary for most people. In many situations where routine procedures must be carried out over and over again, it is better to prepare a checklist than rely on memory. This is as true for preparing a plane on take-off as it is for using a complicated photocopier.

Knowledge can be acquired by observing, listening, reading – indeed, by using all of our senses. For most of us this knowledge must stimulate our interest, appear important and fit into some kind of pattern to be retained. People learn not when they are confronted with information, but when they react to it. Without this reaction little learning takes place.

Helping someone to acquire a skill has been described above, but to be fully effective the person must want to acquire this skill. The skill may be of intrinsic interest or it may help someone to achieve other goals (higher grade, more pay, increased job satisfaction). Interest and a desire to learn can be enhanced by making the learning programme itself interesting and rewarding.

Helping people to understand is more demanding. People learn to understand when they think things through for themselves. Thus, rather than presenting someone with an algorithm for a process, it is better to get that person to work out the algorithm for themselves. Instead of presenting people with clear-cut arguments in favour of a course of action, it is better to have a discussion where alternatives are posed and the advantages and disadvantages are explored. In fact, many skills are better taught by this 'discovery' method, as the person becomes more flexible and able to vary his actions as the situation varies. An individual who learns in this way can cope with the unusual situation and a new demand more readily than can people who perform skills by rote.

'People learn to understand when they think things through for themselves.'

Empowerment involves people having more understanding and more discretion. It is worth while taking time to ensure that your training and development methods support this approach. Much of the learning required in organizations can be anticipated and planned (this is described next). However, there is much to learn that cannot be classified or planned. The ongoing learning that can occur in a dynamic way as the organization develops is discussed below.

Planned learning

It is easy to spend a fortune on training and development, but how can you ensure that this expenditure is well directed? This problem can be tackled at two levels: strategically or operationally (see Chapter 13). The strategic approach involves identifying priorities for the organization by linking training and development activities to the business plans of the company. The operational approach is to take each task or job as a subject of study and then develop an appropriate training programme based on these to equip individuals to perform well.

Planned learning using either of these approaches may be essential where there are identifiable skills that must be acquired or 'bought in' if the company is to survive. In most countries there are a number of occupations and occupational activities that people without the requisite qualification or licence are not allowed to perform. These restrictions mostly relate to health and safety, either of the workers or the public at large. The subjects range from airline pilots to fork-lift truck drivers and transport managers.

The analysis may also highlight areas where there may be potential weakness in the future as new technology is introduced, demanding new skills, or as experienced staff retire or leave for other reasons. Therefore, those planning training need to look ahead at the levels of staff required and the skills they will need, in relation to current staffing levels and anticipated staff turnover.

Dynamic learning

There is another, complementary way of approaching learning in organizations. This views organizations as a collection of 'systems' that form a cohesive whole. It may be worth while to look at information flows and material flows within the company. Equally it is worth investigating causes and effects more deeply, and side-effects as well. If sales are falling, what are the causes and what are the alternative strategies for coping? All too often thinking in this area has, in the past, been superficial. Off-the-cuff instinctive reactions such as reducing the price can prove counter-productive if the customers are choosing a product with different characteristics rather than choosng it because of its price.

'Organizations that fail to learn from their mistakes are condemned to repeat them.'

Organizations that do not delve more deeply into why problems occur fail to learn from their mistakes and are condemned to repeat them. In a learning organization, assumptions are surfaced, problems are analyzed and underlying mechanisms explored. Otherwise, sometimes actions that have a long lead time before the effects are felt can be overlooked.

As people in organizations start to work together to solve problems they learn from each other. They build up shared learning experiences and develop a dynamic learning culture. In this culture the methods used in systematic training come alive. People develop a thirst for knowledge and skills. The motivation to learn transforms the training and development experience. The lack of enthusiasm for learning – so often a real stumbling block in traditional training activities – is removed.

As people within organizations dig more deeply into how things work out, these shared 'mental models' help in the decision-making and the decision-sharing processes. Coupling this shared thinking process with a corporate vision, capable people and effective teamwork is a winning combination (these ideas are explored in more detail in Chapter 15).

Coaching, counselling and mentoring

You will recall that we mentioned coaching and counselling at the end of Chapter 6. Some people do not draw a distinction between these two words. Often the two processes are interwoven in the same interview session.

Coaching

'Coaching' is concerned with helping another person to acquire a skill or knowledge and understanding that the 'coach' already possesses. The term is commonly used in sport where a coach helps an athlete or a player to improve. In the world of industry, commerce and the public sector, the word is more commonly used to describe the process of helping someone to do better at his job by observing the person in action and offering the learner advice and guidance. The help may take the form of a boss setting her subordinate more demanding tasks and providing support as she tackles them. It may take the form of the manager asking questions of the learner that are aimed at helping the individual to think things through more clearly, consider more options, explore possible outcomes of decisions. In each case, we assume that the coach has knowledge, skill or experience to pass on to the trainee.

Increasingly we find managers who know less about the process, the product or the technology than their subordinates. This is not a problem, provided managers are themselves prepared to learn from their subordinates and be coached by them. The concept of an all-seeing, all-knowing manager who can do every job as well as his people is an anachronism – if it ever was true. The point here is that managers in empowered organizations have no hesitation in learning from subordinates. They are, after all, sentient beings capable of logical thought and valuable insights.

In most organizations, managers are not going to work well together if they do not understand the basic needs and concerns of their colleagues. They must spend time together and learn from each other. One of the advantages of empowerment is that the 'troops' can be left to get on with the job while managers attend to other matters, such as closer cooperation and looking to securing the future.

Counselling

'Counselling' involves helping someone to make a decision about the way they will behave in future or how they will cope with a problem. We counsel someone when they, and they alone, can decide. We cannot decide for them.

We are accustomed to using the word counselling in relation to the problems that people face outside work. People who run into marriage problems or who suffer the bereavement of a loved one can sometimes be helped by someone who will simply listen. However, in the work context, too, we may be confronted by someone who is experiencing such an emotional problem. There are experts who are better equipped to deal with this than managers generally are, but managers have to cope in the meantime.

Often, people in organizations have decisions to make about work. Will they seek a transfer, promotion, a place on a course? If these are all genuine options, the person should be free to make up her mind. What can the 'counsellor' do in this case? First of all she must listen. She will seek to help the individual to consider all the people involved, explore the options, seek further information, if necessary. She may make suggestions – tentatively – and relate relevant experiences. She will not tell the individual what to do, if she is a true counsellor.

Mentoring

'Mentoring' is the term used to describe a process whereby one person helps another in his personal, usually career, development. A mentor may be a senior person in an organization who is asked to maintain contact with a graduate recruit over the first few years of his employment with the company. There may be no reporting relationship involved. The graduate works in a different part of the organization. The mentor will see the graduate from time to time, seek information about how he is developing, what challenges have been encountered.

The mentor will seek to ensure that the graduate learns from these events. If the mentor considers that the graduate needs to be exposed to new experiences, he may approach the appropriate authorities and support the graduate by facilitating a transfer to a new situation. The mentor will help the graduate to plan his personal development and provide advice and guidance based on his own knowledge and experience. The role of mentor has elements of counselling, coaching and more, especially regarding the opening of doors.

However, this is not the only kind of mentor. A manager can be a mentor to her subordinates. She can take an interest in each individual, coaching them in their jobs, providing new challenges, counselling them in relation to their future development and opening doors – including transfers out of their domain. Because of the interpersonal nature of the process, sometimes a boss–subordinate mentor relationship does not work well. The solution depends on the circumstances, but may include a transfer or the boss asking a peer to act as mentor to one of her people. In an open and honest empowered organization, this should pose no problems.

There are some situations in which a set of managers is responsible for a group of supervisors and their people, but where the duties are such that no supervisor meets a particular manager very often. In such cases, a simple boss–subordinate relationship does not exist. We know of instances where the allocation of, say, four or five supervisors to each manager for mentoring works. This does mean that the managers must be prepared to exchange information and a supervisor must be able to request a transfer if the relationship does not work out in practice.

Appraisals

Managers in command and control cultures are rarely motivated to spend time on this process. In spite of all the training and fine words, the process can become mechanical, forced and patchy in its effectiveness. In this type of culture, some managers see the process more in terms of controlling their subordinates than a way of developing them. Those organizations that succeed in making a success of their appraisal systems are those in which senior managers consider the development of managers to be an important part of the job.

Traditionally, an appraisal is an assessment carried out by a manager on one of her subordinates. This is usually followed by an appraisal interview. In this interview the boss informs the interviewee of her opinion of the individual's performance over the past period (typically one year) and they discuss this together. The discussion then moves on to the future and the manager seeks to gain the interviewee's agreement on how performance is to improve in the future. In practice, both the appraisal and the interview take many forms, but bound up in the process is the fact that several objectives are being pursued.

Typically, the interview offers a formal opportunity to consider matters that ought to have been discussed from time to time during the year, perhaps on an informal basis. In addition, it offers to the interviewee a formal occasion to obtain feedback on past performance. To assure a level playing field, the manager's boss is usually involved in the process – for example, by seeing the appraisal document before and after the interview. Often, the assessment is made against a set of behavioural categories and performance is measured alongside a set of objectives agreed earlier in the year or at the previous appraisal.

In some cases, the process is complicated by the fact that the interviewee is rewarded on the basis of this assessment. This can cause the interviewee to become defensive, finding reasons for any shortcomings and being unwilling to discuss any personal weaknesses that might diminish his reward. Such an atmosphere is not conducive to the most important part of the appraisal process –

seeking future improvements. For this reason, where reward is involved, it is common to have another appraisal, after the dust has settled from the merit award, to consider development.

The developmental aspect of the appraisal process focuses on the future, on the way the business and the operation will develop over the coming months. Both the manager and the interviewee have an interest in improving the unit's performance and in working together to achieve this. In an empowered organization, they can openly discuss what has happened, not seeking to find fault or to ascribe blame, but seeking to learn from these experiences. They may both have something to learn. They can discuss this and how the learning may be achieved.

'Give feedback on performance.'

Consideration can be given to widening the scope of the appraisal, involving more of the people who relate to the interviewee in the work context. There may be people other than the boss, the manager and the boss' boss who have a role to play in the assessment. Some organizations have introduced '360 degree' appraisals. These involve asking for appraisals from all the people who deal with the manager concerned, the boss, subordinates, peers, and people in other sections who deal with the individual concerned. It would be difficult to envisage this working without a high degree of trust between all those involved. As nobody is concerned with apportioning blame (except in extreme circumstances) there is no need to be defensive.

Traditionally, appraisal systems have operated mainly at management and supervisory level. More recently, however, the process has been simplified and employed to cover the whole workforce. In teamworking, it is common practice for every team member to be assessed and given feedback on performance.

Progress checklist

Tick the following items when you can honestly answer 'Yes' to the question posed.

Have you considered how education, training and other aids to learning can be incorporated into your organization's activities? ❏

Have you decided the extent to which you want to explore planning your organization's learning? ❏

Have you recognized that organizations have a corporate learning capacity? ❏

Have you considered how to improve coaching and counselling in your organization? ❏

Can you envisage how mentoring could be incorporated into your organization? ❏

Are you satisfied that any appraisal arrangements are used positively for the improvement of the operation? ❏

13

Planned learning

Planning learning to achieve organizational goals

- Plan training to enable the organization to achieve its objectives.

- Involve all of your people in the process of deciding on learning needs.

- Consider the power of open learning.

- Plan to develop your managers so they have the skills to implement empowerment.

- Formal training methods have a place, used flexibly.

- Monitor the effect of training and development on the organization.

> **Snapshot** *Over a decade ago, a company that manufactured machine parts and tools had a bad patch and lost many employees in the process. The management considered the remaining employees and the site to be capable of renewal. The plant had become outdated, however, and the company decided to invest in new, computer-controlled equipment.*
>
> *Orders for the company's products were sought and found, and so they decided to invest in their people. The manager and his team had a clear grasp of the forward thrust of the company, the technology to be used and the people development that would be needed.*
>
> *The sales and commercial staff were given training in telephone skills, and they spent time on the shop floor to gain an understanding of the problems that people faced there. Training in product knowledge and computer systems was augmented by development of good communication skills, both spoken and written. Coaching was used to underpin learning about preparing quotations and ensuring that customer needs were met.*
>
> *Each employee was assessed annually and the discussion used as a positive springboard for personal development, in terms of job enrichment as well as training.*
>
> *In production control and purchasing, procedures were documented, staff trained and the results recorded. Staff were encouraged to make occasional visits to suppliers to see how components were made and to make contact with people who might later smooth the way when business was transacted. In the manufacturing section, on-the-job instruction was managed well and job rotation used to encourage worker flexibility. Skills enabling staff to know how to use the information supplied by the computer systems and to manage the computer control systems were made integral to the learning process.*
>
> *In the warehousing and distribution areas, coaching was widely used to supplement more formal training. Workers were trained to recognize components and understand how they were used, not just to regard them as a 'number'.*
>
> *Many people also attended relevant external courses. In every section, the link between learning and business activity was recognized and, over a ten-year period, the company became an outstanding success.*

Planning means looking ahead and making the best decisions you can today in the light of what might happen tomorrow. Thus, any plan is drawn up on the basis of a series of assumptions. Those who lead the organization must recognize that if circumstances change, the assumptions may change and the plan will need to be updated and modified accordingly.

The purpose of planning learning is to ensure, as far as possible, that each employee is clear about what is expected of them and that they know how to do their jobs properly and safely. It is part of the job of every director, manager and supervisor to see that people working for them are informed, educated, trained and, where appropriate, given other help in developing their abilities.

Strategic planning

It makes sense to link training and development with the objectives of your organization. There are five key elements in a sound training and development plan.

1 *Outline the future of the business*, especially any changes anticipated over a two- to five-year period – longer in some industries. Be specific about changes you envisage happening in the next 12 months. Take into account all the normal business parameters – what do you expect to sell, how much, to whom and of what quality, how will you sell and deliver your goods and services? It is also essential to include such factors as the introduction of new information systems, new working methods and procedures. Include any factors that will change the work people are required to do and the way they will relate to each other in the work context. Remember that changes in computer systems and quality assurance systems will have an impact on the work of a very large proportion of the workforce – probably everybody! What will be the learning implications of the move towards increasing empowerment?

2 *The demands on people* – how future plans will impact on specific sections and groups of people. What will be expected of them? In broad terms, what knowledge and skills will they need to acquire to achieve the company's goals effectively? It is important to take full account of information flows, where people will have access to new information and where they can make new kinds of decisions – especially as the organization moves towards greater empowerment. It is particularly important to manage the changeover from one situation to another, and to take these transitional situations into account in training and development programmes. Include in this assessment, items derived from the normal day-to-day activity where learning needs are identified by management and workers (see below).

3 *Plans for people development* – outlining the methods to be used to help people to acquire the new skills they need. The methods may include on-the-job instruction and coaching, secondments and transfers, individual and team projects, job-swaps and, where appropriate, internal or external off-the-job learning, seminars, courses and workshops. Where external resources are to be used, identify these. Resources for open learning abound, but care must be taken to ensure that these meet your specific needs.

4 *Resources* must be identified and management commitment to these costs secured. Some of the resources will be external and there will be readily identifiable costs associated with these. If the organization has internal training resources, these costs can be assessed. These internal resources may include trainers, a training centre and learning aids. However, the major cost will be the time that managers and supervisors give to helping themselves and their people to develop. Are they prepared to give this time? Do they see it as a key part of the job, and one against which they will be judged? Where on-the-job training forms a major part of the programme, consideration must be given to the training skills of those who give instruction.

5 *Evaluation* must be considered, looking first at what was achieved during the past year. Then, anticipating that your business plans will succeed, consider what benefits you seek from the training and development activity. For example, are you looking for tangible outcomes, such as improved productivity, lower labour turnover or absentee rates and suchlike? Are you seeking to implement new systems with minimum disruption to the business? Perhaps you hope for less tangible, but nevertheless valuable gains, such as improved commitment from the workforce, an eagerness to accept challenges and embrace improvements in working practices? When the management group can express in clear terms what it is hoped will be gained from training plans, it can set about assessing these benefits and training will work. You will also need to decide how you will monitor progress. It is of limited value to attempt to evaluate a programme after the event if you did not define the aims and institute monitoring activities at the outset.

If you have a business plan, this will form the natural starting point for your analysis of the future learning needs of the business. If you do not have a business plan, you may have to draw up a new document that indicates the way you intend to develop the business. This should cover the next few years – in terms of markets, customers, technology, products and services. In some industries, organizations may need to look many years ahead, both in business planning and in ensuring an adequate supply of trained personnel, for example airline pilots and master mariners.

By studying the business plan, you can usually identify areas of knowledge and skill that are essential for future success. Indeed, any sound business plan includes a list of the key areas of expertise required to achieve success and the measures required to secure those areas of knowledge and skill. Does your company rely on its competitive edge in terms of the technology it uses or the specialist skills of its professional people? Are the skills of your salespeople crucial to success? Do you rely heavily on cash flow and need to ensure that your billing and debt collection are efficient? Are the manufacturing costs crucial?

Trace the various processes of your operation to find crucial areas, including, as appropriate:

- market intelligence gathering
- research and development of new products and services
- recruitment and selection of staff
- ordering of raw materials
- manufacture
- storage and distribution
- marketing and sales
- information flows
- inventory control
- the delivery of goods and services
- invoicing and receipts.

You and your colleagues may be able to add to this list some headings for your own organization. Now consider carefully whether or not you have the people with the skills you need to take the business forward in each critical area. Do some people need new skills or do the skills they have need updating? If you have neglected training and development in the past, you may find the list daunting, but the trick is to focus on priorities.

Draw up a plan of action with key dates, methods, resources, costs. Detail when you will expect to have reports on progress. Each training programme will have its own objectives, stated in terms of what the trainees will know and be able to do as a result of the programme. We use the word 'validation' to describe checking whether these objectives have been achieved. Evaluation is a more difficult idea. It means making some sort of estimation as to whether or not the training contributed to the success of the organization. In large organizations this process can become bureaucratic, but there are some skills that take time to develop and such planning is helpful.

In planning to become a more empowered organization, one of the areas of concern is the flexibility of your staff. Over time, this means that people will need to learn to perform a wider range of tasks than is required in a command and control culture. You will recall that a characteristic of an empowered organization is that people are prepared to do any job that needs to be done, provided they are capable of doing it effectively and safely. Strict demarcation lines between jobs have no place in an empowered organization.

'People will need to learn to perform a wider range of tasks.'

One of the tricky parts of the process is finding out what each individual needs to learn. In an organization of any size, the top-down approach implied earlier will need to be supplemented by information derived from each individual, especially where the nature of the work is changing. In many cases, this can only be achieved by a series of interviews cascading down the organization to include every worker. In most cases such interviews will be required every year.

Organizations that have introduced this procedure report that the initial response from the workforce is favourable. In effect, it is extending the appraisal system (see below) to the whole workforce.

Open learning

'Open learning' methods offer particular advantages, but the evidence is that unless the company is prepared to invest in proper learning facilities and support, these will not materialize. Open learners require the support of people who will help them to plan their learning, organize their time – including time spent with their families. They need to organize their learning 'space', to lay out their books and papers. They need to decide the learning strategies that work for them and to stick to these strategies.

Adults who learn on a part-time basis benefit from having contact with other learners struggling to master new skills. The other learners may be studying some totally different topic, but that is not the point. It is not difficult to provide subject matter support on the telephone or via computer links. The real problem that adult learners have to contend with is how to manage their time and environment so that learning becomes possible.

Many learners find that a physical facility on site is a great help. It is a quiet place to go, for example at the end of their shift or, better still, an hour or two before the shift starts. It may be equipped with desks, and chairs, books, study packs, video players, computers and telephones, as appropriate. Include a place where a few learners can get together for a chat.

The provision of learning facilities is included in the training and development plan. If you are planning to develop an empowered organization, do not be afraid to include opportunities for people to learn what they want to learn, irrespective of the technical content.

Moral support and encouragement is more readily organized in an empowered organization where people are keen to help each other to develop and improve.

Management development

A crucial area is management development. It is common nowadays to focus on 'competencies'. It is true that there is a basic tool kit of knowledge, skills and abilities that managers need to survive and prosper. If they are seeking a qualification of some sort, acquiring this basic tool kit can prove its own motivation to improve. For managers in full-time employment, methods of learning that relate to the current and prospective jobs often prove highly motivating.

'Many people using open learning methods find that a physical facility on site is a great help.'

Management development, however, cannot be left to formal programmes. The 'formation' of effective managers owes a lot to the influence of the people they work for and the challenges they have to face on the job. In an organization of any size, young managers need mentors who will help them to acquire a variety of experiences and to work for a number of bosses (see Chapter 12). Managers with such breadth of experience are highly valuable in developing an empowered organization.

Once again, the requirements of an empowered organization mean that you will need to consider how to assist managers to learn the management and leadership skills required in this culture (see Chapter 16 for a description of the role of management in this context).

In many organizations, management development has two distinct elements. First, the competencies required for each type of management job are identified and a series of programmes organized. Managers who aspire to become more effective and to secure promotion attend these programmes to develop specific areas of knowledge and skill, in some cases linked to qualifications. Second, alongside this provision, many organizations promote management development by means of an appraisal system.

In an empowered organization, managers do not operate in a vacuum. Management teamwork is of crucial importance and there are a number of activities that can be used to enhance team performance (see Chapter 15).

Training for the task

The technology of breaking down jobs into discrete tasks, identifying the learning required and designing training to meet those needs is all well documented. Indeed, this approach underpins quality management. Here the needs of customers provide the starting point. On this basis, the products and services are specified. The various tasks required, at each stage, to provide these goods and services are itemized. The people are trained to perform these tasks. Within the organization this quality management starts with the people who place the orders for raw materials and equipment, but goes on to embrace the people who actually deliver goods and services to the customer.

The problem with this type of analysis is that it works well when the individual worker has little discretion over what to do next and how to do it. In many jobs, the proportion of work of this nature is diminishing. The discretionary part is on the increase (in Chapter 14 we discuss job concepts in more detail). The classical job analysis, task analysis and training specification need to be used flexibly.

In an empowered organization, people need to learn how to interpret information to make decisions, work flexibly in a team context, think about what they are doing and be alert to opportunities to improve the performance of the company.

Monitoring and evaluating results

It is not difficult to find out whether or not a specific piece of training has achieved its objectives – provided these are stated in behavioural terms. All you can do via training is help somebody to acquire knowledge, understanding and skill that enables them to perform a task. If they can show that they can perform the task(s) specified, the training has been successful in these terms. The term 'validation' is used to describe this process, and the testing of trainees is one element of monitoring.

However, the real question is whether or not the training helped the company in some way. We call that 'evaluation'. The problem with evaluation is twofold. The first is that once someone has been trained, there is no guarantee that they will continue to use that skill properly and consistently. In simple terms, there are three factors that determine how someone behaves at work – their:

- ability
- circumstances
- motivation.

The second problem is that the behaviour of employees is only one (albeit a major) factor in the success of the enterprise. Without the proper tools, raw materials, information and working conditions, people cannot achieve the best results. The provision of a supportive working environment and the motivation of the workers at all levels are key management responsibilities.

This means that assessing the value of training and development is always a matter of judgement. The basis of that judgement can be improved by ensuring that the anticipated gains are described in the beginning and that these gains are sought over time. Monitoring training involves more than keeping track of how many people attend courses or spend time on on-the-job training, and then testing whether or not the training is valid. It involves setting out, in advance, the changes expected in performance operationally, and the behaviour that will deliver that improvement. It requires effort to monitor the extent to which observable behaviour is changing and the performance improvements which are being achieved.

Progress checklist

Tick the following items when you can honestly answer 'Yes' to the question posed.

Do you have a plan to meet your organization's major learning needs to support its anticipated activities? ❑

Have you considered the role of open learning in your organization's learning plans? ❑

Are you confident that your management development procedures will deliver the quality of managers you need? ❑

Have you taken steps to ensure that appraisal methods support the empowered organization? ❑

Are your arrangements for the training of people to perform tasks effective and flexible? ❑

Have you put effective monitoring procedures in place? ❑

Do you have clear objectives for your learning activities in terms of improvements in the performance of the organization as well as the behaviour of the workforce? ❑

14

Empowering individuals

Ways and means to help your people to grow

- Be aware that empowered people need different job concepts.

- Develop people's abilities to contribute to the business.

- Provide opportunities and delegate authority.

- Attend to front-line and middle management problems.

- Secure cooperation and commitment.

Snapshot *Harry, a supervisor, was a bit of a clown. The more people laughed at his antics, the more he would act up to amuse people. This did not interfere with his work – he still did his job properly. But, over time, people came to ignore his comments and suggestions. They thought of them as coming from someone who did not seem to take life seriously. He was working in a situation where the work was dominated by procedures.*

The time came when the organization had to become more cost-conscious. The company decided to train its managers as mentors and its supervisors were each given small projects to do – to improve the operation, and as a learning experience. Workshops were then held where the supervisors were each required to bring the data they had assembled on their projects, prepare their report and present their recommendations to a senior manager.

On the first day, it became clear to Harry that the project he had been given was trivial compared to that of his colleagues. That night he went home and thought out a way to enhance the project to give it more impact and significance. With the help of the tutors, the final report and recommendations were impressive and the senior manager was astounded at the quality of the report and the manner in which the supervisor presented his findings. In his final review Harry remarked 'I am not such an idiot as I thought I was!'

The experience of the project, the support of the workshop and the opportunity to contribute to improving the business had transformed his self-image. It had also enhanced the esteem in which he was held by his colleagues and senior managers. Harry was only one of many managers and supervisors who became empowered by taking part in this project-based training and development programme. The programme gave a fresh impetus to the business.

Empowering people can be dangerous. If you fail to gain their commitment and loyalty, their empowerment may damage the organization. Empowered individuals may outgrow the opportunities in the company. You may need to face these issues squarely before you proceed too far. Many senior managers are content to allow empowered individuals to leave, if there really is no place in the organization for their talents. They argue that such people give enormous value while they are undergoing personal development.

'Empowering individuals can be dangerous if you fail to gain their commitment and loyalty.'

Empowering people has emotional as well as intellectual elements. Empowerment recognizes:

- people's intelligence as well as their labour
- the individuality of each person as well as his employment status
- the aspirations of the individual as well as his efforts.

Empowering individuals involves looking at the jobs they do and the skills they need. Once these are clearer, training and development activities are followed by providing opportunities and yielding authority to the individuals concerned.

Empowering individuals also means recognizing that they are whole people with lives outside the workplace. It means considering the effect of demands at work on their homes, their families and their other interests – and vice versa. It means that the organization must not make unreasonable demands. We all recognize that there will be periods when there is pressure to perform, but the burdens must not be too great or the pressure excessively prolonged.

'Empowering individuals means recognizing that they are whole people.'

Job concepts

The job concept is changing. Empowering individuals also involves looking again at people's jobs. In a command and control culture, jobs are viewed as collections of tasks that normally fill up the working day. Using work study techniques, any time not used on tasks may be considered as wasted, and be filled with more tasks. Jobs are defined in great detail in this way. Such techniques have been applied up to supervisory level, but rarely to management where there is a greater degree of freedom in the use of time. Indeed, two managers in ostensibly similar jobs can use their time quite differently, but still be successful.

With the widespread dispersal of information, the growth in automation and the rapidity of change, precise job definitions no longer make sense. In an empowered organization, people must learn to come to terms with less well-defined jobs, but with more sharply defined outcomes of joint endeavour. An individual's job in an empowered organization may be considered, in simple terms, to have three parts. There are several tasks that must be performed, and there may also be a precise description of how these 'essential tasks' must be performed by the individual.

Outside these essential tasks, there may be a number of discretionary activities. These may be tasks that the job-holder may do when she can fit them into her timetable, such as simple maintenance tasks relating to machinery used. Some tasks may be optional, expected, but not required. For example, she may want to do some work to improve herself or to enhance her job performance or to improve liaison with a member of her team or another team.

A worker wandering off to talk to someone in another section would raise eyebrows in a command and control culture, but this would be normal in an empowered structure. This means that there may be merit in making sure that there is indeed space and time for people to think and talk to each other. It is counterproductive, therefore, to reduce the number of employees to the absolute minimum necessary for routine operations. Space and time is needed by people to innovate, develop themselves and improve the operation on a continuous basis just is not there.

Beyond this personal responsibility for essential and discretionary activities, many people in empowered organizations find themselves members of operational and, often, project teams. Here their responsibility is shared with a group of people. They have shared goals and it does not matter much which member of the team carries out which task, provided she is competent to do the task. One team member may do the same task or set of tasks most of the time. Another may do a variety of tasks from day to day. The point is that the goals are achieved. We might call this part of the job 'shared tasks'.

Thus, the empowered employee may have a job with these three parts:

- essential tasks
- discretionary activities
- shared tasks.

The mix of these three elements will depend on the nature of the operation. Some jobs cannot be shared – for example, because there is not enough work for more than one person. The lone telephone operator in a smaller firm cannot 'share' the telephone call he is taking, although there are ways in which operating the telephone exchange can be shared. The van driver who delivers goods or the taxi driver on call cannot share her work once she has left the depot. If she is a member of a team of drivers they may be able to find ways to work well together in planning their routes and working hours. In the case of deliveries from a distribution centre, the complexity of the delivery schedules normally means that these are worked out by the transport manager on a computer. However, there is generally some scope to take the driver's views into account.

In other jobs, the scope for activities beyond the essential tasks may be limited. For example, bank staff operating modern telephone banking techniques often have little scope for straying outside the defined brief. Equally, an operative in a distribution centre may be set the task of picking goods for delivery to a store. Not much scope here for originality. But such operatives may well have something valuable to say about their jobs, the way the work is laid out or the labelling of goods.

Some jobs can only be done by one person, but involve scope for discretion. A dispatcher responsible for coordinating all the aircraft services required to prepare an airliner for take-off has to follow the critical path closely. His scope for decision making increases dramatically when some problem occurs.

> 'The scope for teamwork and flexibility is often greater than seems possible at first sight.'

The scope for teamwork and flexibility is often greater than seems possible at first sight. A team of aircraft services personnel assigned the task of unloading passenger baggage have little opportunity, at that moment, to vary the way the task is performed. The procedure and the number of people required is prescribed. But if you look at the tasks performed overall by a group of aircraft services personnel, and imagine that they are given the freedom to vary the resources employed, you can see how they could make a very real impact on the business. Aircraft delays are frequent, and when they happen the team can respond by using team members to optimize resources in ways that would be difficult to manage at speed in a rigid hierarchical system.

In a highly automated manufacturing plant, operatives spend time setting up machines and managing changeovers. Such changeovers may be, for example, from one product to another or, in the case of cable manufacture, from one reel of work in progress to the next. Then they monitor the performance of the equipment and step in when any unacceptable deviation appears to be developing. In the past, it was customary to allocate an individual to each machine, but with modern equipment this is rarely necessary. What is needed, though, are teams of operatives who will work together to minimize machine down-time, solve the day-to-day problems that arise, cooperate effectively with other sections and spend time working on improvements.

An individual needs ability, authority and opportunity to become empowered and to operate in this way. Organizations require empowered individuals who are committed to the organization's goals. Management can encourage an individual to acquire knowledge, skills and understanding, but attention must also be paid to that person's desire to learn.

Although the following topics are discussed sequentially, it is important to recognize that several initiatives must occur simultaneously. As individuals develop ability, they must become more involved in discussions and decisions. At the same time, work must proceed on creating the climate that encourages individual commitment to the well-being of the firm. These factors will enhance the motivation to learn and develop.

Developing ability

People learn when they react to what they see, hear and feel. Thus, people need to become involved if they are to learn and develop. Much of the motivation to learn comes from the anticipated outcome. This might be the ability to drive a car, play a tune, operate a machine or master some computer software. The newly acquired knowledge and skill may enable the individual to gain pleasure from the activity or gain some related advantage. He might now be able to visit his girlfriend who lives a distance away, play in an orchestra, do a job well or just earn good money.

'People learn when they react to what they see, hear and feel.'

People learn more when there is pleasure in the learning as well as in the outcome. A training programme that is boring, repetitious or requires long periods of concentration will not prove cost-effective. It needs to engage the learner and provide stimulation, variety and rewards along the way. Such rewards should be in terms of tangible, recognized achievements.

People are often encouraged to learn if there is companionship in the learning. In a group of people learning together, some will grasp particular points quicker than others. It will not always be the same people who learn fast. When those who learn a point fast help their colleagues, and that help is accepted, a learning community develops. The existence of a learning culture, where people are prepared to learn from each other and help each other, is a characteristic of the empowered organization. The development of a community of learning is enhanced when the group is also committed to a common operational goal – the success of the organization.

> **Snapshot** *A group of trainees went on a course in farming. In the group, graduates were mixed with young trainees who had no formal qualifications at all, but had some practical experience.*
>
> *A consultant who went to visit the group expected that this mix of abilities would cause serious problems, but he found that, over the weeks, the trainees had developed respect for each other. The graduates were helping the experienced trainees to understand the theoretical aspects of the course, whilst the youngsters were using their experience to help the graduates acquire some of the practical skills, such as castrating bull calves.*
>
> *The group had developed into a little learning community.*

Learning is essentially about having an experience and reflecting on that experience. In planning to help people to develop, remember that there are different types of learning. In simple terms, knowledge is easy to acquire – and quickly lost unless it is reinforced, especially by usage. Knowledge can be acquired by reading, listening to experts, observing and so forth. Skills take longer to acquire, but stay with people much longer. The skills may be rusty, but often they are still there, years after they have been gained. Understanding requires more thought. It is better to design learning experiences that make people think through the results of action and decisions, rather than present them with solutions (you will recall that these ideas were discussed in more detail in Chapter 12).

These considerations will assist you as you design learning experiences for your people. As people become more empowered, they will want to know more about the company, how it works, its range of products, suppliers, customers. This is mostly factual information – knowledge. People can acquire this by reading and listening to talks. The subject matter can be revised by means of discussion. An empowered organization needs people who are more versatile, having a broader range of skills than is traditionally the case. You may, therefore, need to train up some more on-the-job instructors and to upgrade the skills of your workers.

The empowered organization needs, above all, people who can make decisions and think through the results of their actions. Decision making is a skill that requires understanding to be exercised effectively. You may need to train your managers to lead discussion groups where the decisions made by individual workers and teams are looked at in detail. The aim of such discussions is not to find fault, but to increase understanding of the factors involved, improve the quality of future decisions and foster the development of a learning community.

This learning community concept should begin with the management group. The initial workshops in a management of change programme should have this development as one of their key objectives.

> 'The empowered organization needs people who can make decisions and think through the results of their actions.'

Project work can form an excellent vehicle for helping people to develop. When choosing a team of people to tackle a problem in the organization, you will need to think first of the kinds of people you will need. Consider the expertise they can bring and the interest groups they represent. If it is a large and complicated task, you may also need a competent project leader. For less complicated problems, it may be a learning experience to give this to someone who, with suitable coaching and support, could do a sound job.

You may now consider whether or not there is anyone who could be included in the team mainly because it will be a useful learning experience for him or her. This may influence your choice of expert or interest group representative or the person may have some other attribute to bring. Do not add someone who will merely be a make-weight – the 'learner' must also be a contributor. Sometimes this person may be quite ignorant of the subject matter, but this may not be a bad thing. If she is intelligent, then the 'idiot' questions she asks may well trigger some lateral thinking or cause some pre-conceptions to be re-examined.

The interplay of people from different backgrounds and with different expertise tackling a problem together is a valuable learning experience in itself. It can be enhanced by training those in the project group to review the way they work and the learning they have achieved from time to time.

In an empowered organization, any formal training will be supplemented by coaching, counselling and, in some cases, mentoring. Formal and informal appraisals will also form part of the environment within which people will develop. Coaching occurs when one individual helps another to acquire a skill. Counselling occurs when one individual helps another to make a decision that only he can make.

Often the two processes are interwoven in a discussion, but it is helpful for the coach to understand the differences between the two processes. Counselling is particularly important when, for example, an individual has to make a decision about some aspect of her personal development or the direction she wishes to go. It is the individual who must make such a decision. The counsellor can help the individual to think things through properly, to consider alternatives, implications and possible outcomes.

The term 'mentoring', you may recall, is used to describe a situation where one individual takes a particular interest in another person's development, offering coaching, counselling and opportunities. In some organizations, a selection of senior managers act as mentors for young managers or graduate trainees. This method has also been used to help potentially disadvantaged people. By seeing them from time to time, they can help them to face any difficult decisions. Because of their influence, they may be able to help ensure that the graduate has opportunities to develop within the organization. In such schemes, the graduate is rarely responsible to his mentor as a manager. The mentoring is 'off-line', as it were.

Other organizations have taken the concept of mentoring as far as possible, and encouraged each manager to act as mentor to his people. The mentoring relationship depends on a degree of personal rapport. In some cases, the line manager may not have a rapport with one of his people and this individual may be assigned an alternative mentor. In an empowered organization, coaching, counselling – and even mentoring – need not be confined to managers (for more details, see Chapter 12).

Equal opportunities

Organizations today find that within their ranks are people who, through no fault of their own, find themselves at a disadvantage in the internal employment market. We are all guilty of some measure of prejudice and this can easily intrude into the day-to-day decisions made in the workplace. Race, gender and disability can, even today, cloud judgement. There is no place for such discrimination in an empowered organization, and there are several steps that can be taken to help people who are at a disadvantage. Some people are educationally disadvantaged. For example, although they may have a reasonable level of intelligence, for some reason their literacy and numeracy skills are underdeveloped.

Each organization will need to examine the problems faced by any disadvantaged groups in its employ and take steps to remedy the situation. In most cases, it is a long haul. Senior and middle managers may need to think through their own positions, and perhaps be helped by specific training programmes. The disadvantaged themselves may need to be helped by positive action programmes, including mentoring and assertiveness training. The organization may need to examine the position from the disabled person's viewpoint. Is there wheelchair access? Can job aids play a part? There are specialist organizations that can help senior managers grappling with these problems.

> **Snapshot** *As part of its efforts to become a leading authority in London (see the first Snapshot in Chapter 15), Lewisham Council has taken a particular interest in equal opportunity issues. The Council has monitored its 10,000-strong workforce for race and gender annually since 1983, and from 1994 included the disabled too. The data has highlighted areas where action is needed to reduce the under-representation of women, black or disabled staff relative to the local community served by the Council.*
>
> *Measures to combat under-representation of disabled people include a specially designed recruitment advertising campaign, coupled with a 'Hotline'. This has resulted in a number of new appointments of disabled staff across the Authority. A positive action programme has been introduced to help black managers develop their skills and careers within the Authority. Black employees are still under-represented at middle and senior management levels. The key feature of the programme is the sponsor scheme in which senior managers (mostly white) volunteer to act as sponsors (effectively mentors) for junior black managers. Care is taken to match up each manager with a sponsor who can provide appropriate help and with whom the manager being sponsored feels comfortable. The sponsors typically devote some time each week to helping the manager to plan his or her development, providing advice, guidance and information on learning opportunities. The sponsor can also 'open doors', arranging job shadowing, project work and other developmental activities.*

Authority and opportunity

Knowledge, skills and understanding that remain unused tend to fade into the background. Indeed, if someone has taken the trouble to acquire new abilities, it can be frustrating for these to be overlooked. As managers gain more confidence in the ability of the people in their charge, it is vital to ensure that more responsibilities are delegated to them. Opportunities must be created for people to play their part in running and improving the operation. As ever, authority must be delegated as well as responsibility. Rather than deciding and describing this in detail at the outset, it is better for delegation to evolve over a period of time. Responsible behaviour will be rewarded with increasing authority.

It generally falls to front-line managers to delegate – or, as they may see it, give up some decisions. In so doing they may feel a loss of power and influence. Senior managers must recognize this and take action to deal with it. In a management of change programme moving towards empowerment, there are effectively only two methods. One is to widen the scope of the manager's job. In many organizations that operate as command and control cultures, many of the forward-looking tasks that managers should be concerned with are left undone because managers spend their time fire-fighting. In the move to empowerment, senior managers can insist that front-line managers attend to these tasks.

The second is that, if there are not enough tasks of this kind requiring attention, the organization must reduce the number of managers in areas where operatives have the responsibility and make more decisions. Senior managers must be careful in the way that this is undertaken. It is not easy to maintain a reputation for openness, honesty and trust when you have to make supervisors and managers redundant. You will need to work out what management structures you need, fill the new posts by overtly fair and sensible methods, and be generous to those forced to leave.

'Knowledge, skills and understanding fade into the background, if they are unused.'

As mentioned earlier, jobs may have essential tasks, discretionary tasks and shared tasks. As the organization becomes more empowered, the proportions of these tasks may vary, with increasing emphasis being placed on the discretionary and shared tasks. People will become more conscious of their team roles within operational sections and, hopefully, in the wider context and across shifts, of the inter-relationships between sections and the concept of the whole organization with shared overall goals.

All this will only work when people feel committed to sectional, departmental, site and organizational goals. Trust will be a key factor in achieving this commitment.

Progress checklists

Tick the following items when you can honestly answer 'Yes' to the question posed.

Have you considered the way the nature of jobs will change in the move towards empowerment? ❏

Have you considered how you will set about enhancing the ability of people at all levels in the organization? ❏

Are you seeking to create a learning community? ❏

Are your middle and front-line managers prepared to delegate authority and afford opportunities for people to make meaningful decisions about their work? ❏

It may be useful to use the following checklist to review the ways in which you are helping people to learn. Does your approach meet the following criteria?

Are there rewards for learning? ❏

Is the learning process designed in such a way that it is a pleasurable experience? ❏

Is there companionship in the learning process? ❏

Are there opportunities for experience and reflection? ❏

Are there checklists for key procedures? ❏

Are there opportunities for observation, explanation, practice and constructive feedback? ❏

Are there specific programmes to deal with any problems faced by disadvantaged people? ❏

Is the development of understanding encouraged and discussed? ❏

Is there a process for reviewing decisions as part of the learning experience? ❏

Organizational learning and teamwork

Creating a dynamic learning organization

- View the organization as a total system.

- Develop organization-wide teamwork.

- Learn to understand teamwork processes.

- Develop and share a vision of the company's future.

- Share your understanding of how things work.

- Learn to value and inspire employees.

Snapshot *Lewisham Council is striving to become a model of effective and efficient local government. The Council has taken a number of innovative steps to empower the 10,000-strong workforce. It aims to set quality standards and ensure value for money in its activities. The Council is actively promoting a sense of common purpose and a spirit of cooperation across all its departments.*

A 'learning council' is being created by investing in its people, providing equality of opportunity for career development and striving for continuous improvement in the quality of the services provided. Management development initiatives include corporate self-managed learning programmes for senior managers and special seminars for managers, where high-calibre external speakers address the groups on topical subjects of importance to the Council's work. The use of 360-degree feedback processes have aided the development of the top management teams.

The Council supports employees seeking nationally recognized qualifications and has introduced a comprehensive programme of mentoring schemes, secondments and work shadowing. Special programmes have been arranged to help people potentially held back by discrimination (see the third, final Snapshot in Chapter 14). The Council has also developed an imaginative 'partnership programme' where people with expertise are logged on a register and those who need such expertise can contact them for help. This has led to a number of constructive relationships being formed across departments within the Authority.

The various activities are together helping to transform the original command and control culture into a more team-based and learning-oriented culture. Continued clear direction and leadership from the top is required to nurture this shared sense of purpose and open culture. The investment in people is paying off in terms of improved services that are also value for money.

One of the characteristics of an empowered organization is that learning becomes part and parcel of the way it operates on a day-to-day basis. This goes well beyond the planned learning described in Chapter 12. Several factors work together to produce a learning organization. These may be summarized as follows:

- the holistic view – a view of the organization as a total entity where the various sections and processes interact to produce a set of results greater than the sum of its parts
- developing teamwork across the whole organization; involving everyone
- team processes
- sharing visions and goals
- sharing an understanding of how things work
- valued and aspiring individuals.

The holistic view

In many companies, individual sections see themselves as performing the tasks set for them by management. However, they may give little thought to whether or not these tasks are performed in an optimum way in relation to other parts of the organization. Over and over again you will find that when you start to analyze the way organizations function, you become aware of the fact that they would be far more effective if there was a greater understanding of how the whole thing fitted together and of the underlying philosophy of the company.

Snapshot *A food manufacturing company worked its plant 24 hours a day, 7 days a week for most of the year. It had a complicated shift system to keep the plant running around the clock. Because of the high utilization of the plant and equipment and close control of raw material costs, it was able to pay its employees above the normal rates and still produce its goods at a competitive price.*

On interviewing young managers in the plant, however, it was clear that this basic philosophy had not been explained to them and so they were mystified at some of the decisions taken by management.

Explaining these factors enhanced their commitment to the company. It also enabled them to communicate more effectively with staff and make better decisions in the future.

Every organization operates on the basis of a number of systems. Understanding how these systems work and how they impact each other provides a fundamental way to develop improvements and help the organization to learn. The more people understand these systems and the consequences of particular actions, the more effective the organization becomes. A lack of appreciation of systems thinking often means that decisions are made on the basis of knee-jerk reactions to the symptoms presented, without time being spent on investigating the underlying causes and effects. Typical examples of a failure to investigate causes properly, and to understand the way systems operate, abound in relation to sales and employee motivation.

> **Snapshot** *A company selling commercial equipment could not understand why its product sales were declining as competitors were selling more of their 'poorer quality' products. They continued with product development, improved their quality control and leaned harder on the salespeople – to no effect.*
>
> *When they were persuaded to start listening to the customers, however, they found that what they had seen as improvements in quality were viewed by many customers as unnecessary complications that increased the price without increasing the usefulness of the equipment.*
>
> *This company had failed to recognize that quality is primarily a factor of what the customer wants and is prepared to pay for in a given situation.*

As long as sections are not familiar with what others do and what information they need, they cannot operate in the best interests of the organization as a whole. Salespeople divorced from manufacture, for example, may sell many products, but the product mix may be difficult for the factory to handle.

'People who see their contribution in context will make better decisions and collaborate more effectively with others.'

An organization that aspires to empowerment needs to consider how it can encourage people to take an interest in the *whole* organization. People need to know how it fits together, what it makes and sells, who its customers are and what they look for in the company's products or services. People who can see their own contribution in context will be better at making decisions and collaborating with other sections.

Methods that have been used include exhibitions of products and distributing attractive documentation about the company. Visits to other sections, customers and suppliers may have a place and, in some cases, secondments or transfers to other sections for short periods of time. Joint meetings with other sections or with people on other shifts who work with the same equipment have also proved their worth. In building teamwork it is often better to hold workshops with people drawn from a range of sections. Holding teamwork workshops where everyone comes from the same sections may enhance camaraderie at the section level, but it does little for wider teamwork. Teamwork in sections can readily be developed on the job where the people work together anyway. In developing firm-wide teamwork, there is no great gain to be had from taking the team on a workshop unless there are specific problems to be ironed out.

Snapshot *A local authority in the North of England had a number of sections that interfaced with young people. As time went on, it became clear that, as far as particular young people were concerned, the authority seemed to be working at cross purposes. The plans and policies in one section did not seem to square with those elsewhere in the authority's patch. The problem was how to help each section to understand what others were trying to achieve.*

A decision was made to organize a kind of 'fair' on a given day. Each section was to prepare a stand with pictures and textual material that would illustrate what it was trying to achieve and the methods it was using. Initially, people resented the time taken to prepare for this event, but eventually it went ahead.

On the day, one or two members from each section took charge of their stand. Others wandered around looking at the exhibits and chatting to their colleagues, asking questions, seeking to understand what was going on throughout the borough. During the day, the people staffing the stands were changed to give everybody a chance to visit the other exhibits.

The results were not dramatic, but, over a period, as understanding developed, so their policies became more consistent and the sections become more supportive of each other's work – to the benefit of the young people concerned.

Organization-wide teamwork

The elements of teamwork were described in some detail in Chapter 5, so here we shall just concern ourselves with the methods you can use to enhance teamwork within an organization. You will notice that we are not aiming primarily at identifying specific groups of people to develop into 'teams'. Where a group of people work together to achieve results, then developing teamwork within that group can be helpful. There is, however, the very real danger that such a group can become insular, preoccupied more with its own goals and survival than with the overall good of the organization or with the success of other groups. Teams that are knit too strongly together may find it difficult to accept newcomers. Operationally, the composition of the teams varies from day to day in some situations.

Consider this simple, but proven concept. If people are trained to understand the elements of teamwork and to acquire the necessary skills, teams will form spontaneously, given the right conditions. Our recommendation is that you seek to generate teamwork, as far as possible, throughout the whole organization. The conditions necessary for teamwork include a group of skilled team workers who share a goal, values and perceptions. For the team to contribute effectively to the organization, it is vital that the team's goals are congruent with those of the organization. This simple formula is illustrated in Figure 4.

Figure 4 The teamwork formula

Team processes

When a group of people is allotted a task, several processes come into play. The extent and duration of these processes will depend on the complexity of the task and the extent to which these people have worked together before. The first stage is deciding just what the task is. In many cases, this is not as straightforward as it seems.

Snapshot *A series of five-day training workshops was held for supervisors. Each day, a group of four or five supervisors would be given a task. In each course, there were three or four such groups. The task was to prepare a presentation on a given topic. In order to do this, they had to discuss the topic, gather information, seek a measure of agreement, organize their ideas, prepare visual aids and work out a 'script'.*

Almost every group started out by discussing the topic at length. Late in the day, they would suddenly realize that they had to pull together a presentation. The initial focus was on the topic, not on the task. This meant that they had given inadequate attention to the ordering of the data and the best way to present their ideas and recommendations. The quality of presentations suffered.

As the week proceeded, they learned the discipline of focusing on the task, controlling the discussion, marshalling their ideas, creating effective visual aids and preparing a strategy for presenting their views. This did not diminish the effort made to deal thoroughly with the topic and discuss their points so that they reached a degree of agreement. However the clarity of thought about the task was essential for success. The quality of the presentations improved dramatically, and so did the teamwork.

Another process involves each individual assessing her own potential contribution to the task, and what each of the other members of the team might or might not be able to contribute. This process is ongoing, because people may continue to reappraise these factors in the light of experience. It is as well to recognize where motivation creeps into this situation. If you want team members to give of their best, you must ensure that this is not inhibited by the reward system (see Chapter 4). Individuals must feel that their contributions will be recognized and accepted by other team members. At the same time, you must develop a culture where ideas, suggestions and help are acceptable coming from everybody, not just from the evidently able, intelligent or articulate.

'When a group of people is allotted a task several processes come into play.'

A further process is the sharing of ideas, suggestions and experiences. One of the factors that inhibits effective teamwork is that people often make suggestions based on assumptions that may not be shared by other members of the team. If you want fully effective teams, you will need to encourage people to articulate their assumptions. Questions such as 'Why do you think that will work?' must be posed, and answered, as genuine enquiries, and not as an attack on the person's ideas. It is axiomatic that in preparing a budget every assumption must be stated. The only acceptable explanation of a difference between a figure in a budget and the actual expenditure incurred is that the situation has changed, relative to the original assumptions. For example, the price of petrol has risen more than anticipated when the budget was prepared. In the same way, when solving problems and making proposals, people need to question the assumptions that lie beneath these ideas. The readiness to surface these assumptions and to have them questioned and discussed is a mark of mature teamworking.

The task is opened up by the earlier processes, and this must be followed by a closing down process. The process of selecting which avenues to pursue, which suggestions to follow up, what data to seek, is followed by deciding on the preferred solution, hopefully with measures and markers along the way. Implementation with monitoring, feedback and adjustment ensues. Another mark of effective teamwork is when the team reviews how it has been working, not just what progress has been made.

You can enhance the development of effective teamwork by encouraging teams to review how well they have performed in terms of:

- identifying the task
- sharing ideas and assumptions
- considering alternative actions
- choosing the preferred solution
- planning with measures and markers
- reviewing teamwork as well as achievement.

It is not too difficult to draw up simple questionnaires that aid this process. After using them a few times, the discipline can be embedded in the way people work, without the prop of paperwork. Encouraging such reviews as a way of life within an organization can enhance teamwork.

'Enhance teamwork by reviewing how the team has performed.'

Sharing visions and goals

A team cannot operate without a shared goal. An organization cannot fulfil its potential unless people have a shared idea of where the company is going. Shared goals arise from shared visions. Within organizations, this implies that teamwork rests firstly on the sharing of a vision about what the company or public body is trying to do. Organizations that prepare mission or vision statements hope, by this means, to inspire and energize their own people, as well as present a clear message to their customers and investors.

'People's freedom to raise their concerns with management is a mark of empowerment.'

Although the creation of a mission statement or vision may be the work of one person or of a small board of directors, eventually this must be communicated 'down the line'. Methods for achieving this are outlined in Chapter 5. People need opportunities to discuss this vision and what it means in their own neck of the woods. This process of thinking through, with others, the implications of a mission statement is part and parcel of organization-wide team development.

In a healthy organization, people should be able to see how their own goals and activities fit into this overall picture. They may find that there are activities in which they are engaged or methods they are using that do not support the vision. The freedom they feel to raise these concerns with senior management will be a mark of their empowerment. The validity of the points raised will be a measure of their understanding. The response of senior management will be a test of their commitment to an empowered workforce.

Sharing an understanding of how things work

We all have an idea of how things work in practice and what actions should be taken to put things rights. But somehow, other people do not seem to see it that way. They do not do what we would think of as being sensible in the circumstances. Why is that? It is because other people see things differently? They have a different view of priorities. They have a different opinion about what would happen if our action was taken.

'A lot of fruitless friction could be avoided if assumptions and perceptions were shared.'

When we move from world affairs to what happens in organizations, the same problems arise. We see things differently to the people in charge, and the people who make decisions in other departments. A lot of the fruitless friction in organizations is down to these differences of view. We need to find ways to talk to each other about our assumptions, about the situation and the way things actually work. The problem is that these opinions and perceptions are often bottled up and hidden from view. The resentment is often voiced, but the underlying assumptions remain unquestioned.

These hidden perceptions and assumptions are one of the real stumbling blocks to learning and development. One of the ways in which an organization can deal with this is to consciously encourage people to question, in a constructive manner, some of these assumptions and be prepared to talk about them. Sharing the way we see the way things work with others will lead to a coming together of these perceptions. This means that people will share decisions in a more conscious and committed fashion. At the very least, people will understand one another better and will feel that their opinions have been taken into account. When decisions are made with which they disagree, they will still feel a level of commitment to those decisions.

People who are not committed to decisions play along with the group, going through the motions. They then blame the decision if things do not work out as planned. People who are committed to decisions try hard to make the consequent actions work.

Valued and aspiring individuals

All these ideas will come to nothing if the organization does not value all its employees, encourage them to give of their best and develop their potential to the full. Modern organizations need people who aspire to do a better job, learn more and develop their own roles and contribution to the business.

Progress checklist

Tick the following items when you can honestly answer 'Yes' to the question posed.

Have you and your senior colleagues learned to take a holistic view of the company? ❏

Do you intend to promote organization-wide teamwork? ❏

Do you and your senior colleagues have a shared vision of the organization and its future? ❏

Have you shared this vision with all your employees? ❏

Have you encouraged people within your organization to discuss the vision and how it relates to their own work and vision of the future? ❏

Do you and your colleagues spend time discussing how things work and digging deeper into some of the key problems you face? ❏

Do you and your colleagues value all your employees and seek to encourage their growth and development? ❏

Leading an empowered organization

Developing the leadership you need to succeed

- Learn to recognize the management style in an empowered organization and how this differs from that in a command and control culture.

- Remember, the need to plan and to manage people remains.

- Many of the routine aspects of the manager's job can be delegated.

- Training and helping people to learn assumes greater importance.

- Coordination and continuous improvement become a way of life.

- Identify the specific leadership qualities required.

- Help managers to develop and enhance their leadership skills.

Snapshot

The Manager and Supervisor in a small manufacturing unit had worked in a command and control culture for years. However, now, the firm was introducing single status for all its employees and encouraging teamwork. An external consultant had discussions with them and sought to explain how they would manage in a teamworking environment.

The decision was made that one-day workshops would be held, each involving about 16 workers plus the Manager and Supervisor. The consultant acted as a facilitator at the workshops. At the first workshop, one worker was late attending the first session and clearly wanted to disrupt proceedings. The Manager and Supervisor wanted to step in and deal with this in the classical 'do what you're told' manner. The facilitator restrained them from this action and started the workshop.

As the group tried to make progress, the disruptive individual kept interrupting, asking irrelevant questions, making cynical comments and generally trying to get his colleagues to disown the whole event. The facilitator patiently sought to deal with each interruption in a constructive manner. By the time coffee arrived, the group was fed up with the troublemaker and told him that if he had nothing useful to say, he had better shut up.

The workshop proceeded and later on the troublemaker started to make sensible remarks as he saw that there was no chicanery, no brainwashing and no coercion. He became a constructive member of the group, both at the workshop and on the shop floor. Much more importantly, the Manager and Supervisor had learned their first lesson – the power of the team. From this beginning, their management style was gradually transformed and they became successful in a teamworking environment.

Empowered organizations need leadership and management. The fact that people at all levels are making decisions does not do away with the need for managers. The nature of management changes. The management style and the tools of the trade characteristic of the command and control type of organization will prove a disaster if they are used by any manager in an empowered organization. A different management style and a different set of manage-ment tools are required.

'Empowered organizations need leadership and management.'

Some directors and managers may already have the ability to operate successfully in an empowered structure and to pro-vide the leadership required. Others will need to learn how to manage in this context. If they come into an empowered organization from outside, they will need training and coaching. If they are inside the organi-zation as empowerment develops, they will have the opportunity to acquire the skills required as part of the change process.

Management style

In a command and control culture, the management must:

- plan for the future and set the overall objectives for the organization
- set goals and targets for every activity in the organization
- set out how each task must be done in detail
- provide all the resources necessary for the operation (raw materials, equip-ment, information), monitor it and ensure that these are available at all times when required by the workforce
- ensure that every employee is properly trained to carry out any tasks to be assigned – the employee must be able to complete the task in the proper manner and without risk to health or safety. Monitor the attendance of every employee
- allocate tasks to individual employees at the beginning of each shift and re-allocate people as demands change
- continuously monitor what each worker is actually doing
- monitor the results of the activity continuously
- step in whenever there is a deviation from the prescribed activity or results and decide what action to take

- initiate discipline at the first signs of any problem, and deal with any grievances at source
- coordinate the activity of the various sections in the operation
- attempt to improve the operation.

In an empowered organization, many of these tasks are delegated to the workforce, which releases the managers to deal with the longer-term issues. Consider the list above in relation to an empowered organization.

The directors of an empowered organization must *plan*. They have the overriding responsibility to secure the long-term future of the enterprise. This involves scanning the environment, identifying customers and planning to meet their needs. It involves taking stock of the competition and assessing the potential impact of technology. From these considerations the overall objectives of the company can be determined. For a 'command and control' culture this may be enough, but in an empowered culture, more is required. To gain the commitment of the workforce – so vital to its success – people need a vision of the organization, what kind of organization it should be and how to make it so.

An empowered organization does not just achieve results, it becomes a recognizable entity. People need to know what that entity is. It is characterized not just by what it achieves, but by how this is done, what values are implicit in the way it does business, the way it deals with customers and treats people, the way it views its employees, the community, the environment. It is the role of the directors to provide leadership in creating, disseminating and discussing this vision with the workforce, and maybe projecting it to the world.

The manager in a command and control structure must control resources. She must think through every detail of what must be done, by whom, how and when. The manager in an empowered organization must still set broad goals and monitor performance against targets, but much of the detail can safely be left to competent and committed employees. A system must be set in place for the provision of machinery, equipment and information. If it is not there, members of the workforce will take steps, within their authority, to secure what they require. The manager is called in only when her authority is required – for example, to place an expensive order or arrange an expensive machine overhaul.

In an empowered organization, a manager does not need to allocate staff to tasks at the beginning of a shift – the teams will see to this. She does not need to be concerned with reallocating staff as priorities change – cooperation between the teams will mean this happens as a matter of course as they will have the information and the authority to transfer staff. The manager will not have to intervene every time there is a minor problem – the workforce will sort it out, contacting directly any technical, engineering or information specialists they need to help them. People in specialist areas will respond to requests without reference to their respective bosses – they have that authority.

Training and helping people to learn assumes much greater significance in an empowered organization. It is not enough to train people to do a range of tasks – people have to learn to think. They have to become acquainted with the overall picture and where their activities fit into this whole. They have to learn to cooperate with others and to make decisions themselves and in collaboration with others. Managers have to encourage, support and coach employees in these skills. At the same time, managers must be able to recognize their own limitations and be prepared to listen to the ideas and opinions of their people, and to learn from them.

'The manager in an empowered organization sets broad goals and monitors performance.'

Managers in an empowered organization have a duty to respond to all the legitimate concerns of their people, and to give them feedback on any suggestions and questions raised. In many cases this means pressing for answers from other sections and from senior people. This is all part of the creation of the climate for an effective operation. This takes time and it is one of the prices to be paid to secure and maintain a committed workforce.

If a member of the workforce has a discipline problem or a grievance, in most cases his colleagues will work with him to sort it out. Only if they are unable to help that individual to overcome his problems will it become necessary for the manager to become involved. Effective teamwork means that members of the peer group will support each other – and expect that support from others.

Once an effective system of communication has been established, coordination is not a problem in an empowered organization. People want the whole thing to work and they know this cannot be achieved without effective cooperation. People in an empowered organization want to do a better job and to bring about improvements. Continuous improvement becomes a way of life, people on the shop floor being constantly on the look-out for ways to do the job better. What they cannot do, as a rule, is take ideas from other places and investigate new equipment. They cannot identify needs in the marketplace or devise new products and services to meet these needs. Such activities must be primarily a responsibility of the managers in the organization. Often, however, there comes a time when it makes sense to involve people from the shop floor in this type of work.

Leadership qualities

From the above it is easy to see that managers in an empowered organization need to be leaders of a particular kind. In many organizations, it is helpful to have charismatic leaders who can eloquently explain what the enterprise is about, its character, aims and objectives, but such people are rare. Mostly we need to identify people who have the ability to *develop* leadership qualities and then nurture them.

The manager leads in an empowered organization by setting goals and creating the climate for an effective operation. The qualities we are looking for in empowerment leaders are difficult to encapsulate in words, but the following comments may be helpful.

'Managers in an empowered organization need to be leaders of a particular kind.'

A leader in an empowered organization must have an ability to look ahead and plan to succeed. He must be able to communicate effectively with the people who work for him, especially regarding targets and expectations. He must be able to listen, and not just to the words, but to the depth of feeling behind them. He must be sensitive enough to detect when his people need help. The leader must be able to communicate effectively with those to whom he reports, accurately conveying the results of his section's work and the concerns of his people.

To his people he represents management, and to management he represents his people. He is their defender, ensuring that they are properly equipped, trained, informed and fairly treated. He will act as a coach, sometimes a counsellor, and often a mentor. He will know when to call on extra help – for example, when one of his people has a serious problem. He will have the ability to earn the trust of his people by virtue of his own trustworthy, consistent behaviour and fairness.

He will have the ability to monitor results and give praise and constructive feedback to his people when required. He will have the ability to initiate and carry through the discipline procedure if necessary, but with the rehabilitation of the person being his major goal. He will be sensitive to anyone with a grievance and be able to discern whether or not it is justified. Where appropriate, he will be seen to take action to deal effectively with any genuine grievance.

He will demonstrate a very real concern for the safety and health of his people and anyone who is involved with the work or the areas for which he is responsible. He will not expect any of his people to undertake tasks unless they are able to do the work competently and safely, and they have the proper tools.

Such a leader will be an optimist, seeking excellence in every aspect of his work.

He will be eager to see all his people develop their knowledge and skills to the full. He will be concerned to move ever forward, striving for excellent results – a continuously improving return on investment and service to customers.

Learning to lead

How can we help people to acquire these attributes? In some cases we are talking about specific skills and the initial instruction in these can be given on training courses. For example, planning, target setting, communication, coaching, counselling, mentoring, discipline and grievance handling, health and safety management, quality management can all be covered by courses.

Over and above any formal courses, there are three aids to learning that should be characteristics of an empowered organization:

- mentoring from a senior colleague
- peer coaching
- a supportive culture.

Mentoring has been discussed fully in Chapter 12, so suffice it to say here that, in an empowered organization, it is helpful for each senior manager to act as mentor to the managers who report to her. Very occasionally this is not advisable – for example, if their personalities clash or if the manager is being moved about on a development programme. In these cases, another senior manager may be able to fulfil the role.

A group of managers can agree among themselves to support each other by offering help and advice on a reciprocal basis. If one manager feels a need to discuss an incident or a problem, he can feel free to call on a colleague to act as a sounding board and offer advice. If a manager sees another behaving in an inappropriate manner she may take the opportunity to discuss the incident with her colleague. If the atmosphere is right, and the comments are offered in a constructive manner, this would be acceptable.

If managers are open to comments from their subordinates as well as from their bosses and peers, they often find that this can accelerate their personal development. This assumes that their subordinates are behaving in a responsible manner and that they have learned to be constructively critical. When the workforce recognizes that the managers have to learn and develop as well as themselves, you have the makings of a powerful partnership.

Progress checklist

Tick the following items when you can honestly answer 'Yes' to the question posed.

Have you fully grasped the different style required to manage within an empowered environment? ❏

Are you ready to accord more emphasis to employee training and development? ❏

Have you a clear picture of the kind of leadership required? ❏

Do you have plans to help managers develop the attributes they will require as leaders in such an environment? ❏

PART IV

Next steps

啓発

Facing the future

**Now you must consider what
action you will take**

In this final chapter you are asked to consider carefully the challenges faced by management and your personal response.

In terms of relationships with employees, there are seven key challenges to be faced by most senior managers over the coming years:

1 employment patterns

2 retaining talent

3 core values

4 management style

5 trade unions

6 world trade

7 employee commitment.

Employment patterns

In Chapter 11, we drew attention to the variety of contractual relationships that can exist between individuals and organizations. There are full-time, part-time, permanent, temporary and subcontracted people working side by side in organizations. Their contracted hours may be by the week or by the year or on on a variable basis from week to week. They may be employed by the organization or by an agency or by a subcontractor.

The challenge will be to maintain a wholehearted commitment of all these workers to the firm, its customers and its goals. It is difficult to see how this can be achieved without embracing empowerment.

Retaining talent

The modern mobile labour market makes it easy for talented employees to find alternative employers who will offer more attractive reward packages. This problem is particularly acute in the worldwide financial services sector.

The challenge here is to offer such people rewarding work and a stake in the enterprise as well as a competitive reward deal.

Core values

People in the marketplace becomes confused and then impatient when they perceive inconsistent behaviour in different parts of your organization. Companies that expand rapidly by acquisition are quite likely to encounter marked differences in culture between the components of the new conglomerate.

Ways and means must be found to enable the cultures to cohere, learn from one another and seek best practice across new boundaries. The core values need to be disseminated and discussed to ensure consistency across all the various business relationships involved, as described in Chapter 11.

Management style

The organization's core values must be translated into the management style of the organization, especially the way it deals with people.

Consistency and consideration must be the watchwords. As organizations expand, there is often a need to ensure that opportunities are open for individuals to grow and develop by moving across divisions. It is all too easy for parochialism to stifle the development of managers, which is so vital to the firm's future. The workforce, too, must be viewed as a resource for the *whole* group, not just for the place where they start.

Trade unions

In one way or another trade unions will continue to play an important part in the employment scene. No responsible employer can afford to ignore the need to cultivate constructive relationships with trade unions that have an impact on its operations. This impact may be direct, because the trade union is recognized for bargaining purposes. The impact may be due to the norms it sets for the industry or the political influence the trade union movement has on the activities of multinational bodies, such as the European Union.

Trade unions have a legitimate interest in the welfare of their members. The aim for management must be to work together with trade union members to secure the success of the business and then to negotiate fair deals. And, in the midst of change, the impact on individuals must never be forgotten.

World trade

Few organizations can exist by considering only the local or national marketplace. Goods, services, funds and people now move across the globe.

Differences in culture, employment practices and legal frameworks make it difficult to sustain corporate values across such boundaries.

Employee commitment

Maintaining the motivation of employees in a constantly changing marketplace is perhaps the most demanding challenge of all. Few employees now regard their current employer as the only option. Most would find it difficult to believe that they will remain with that employer for the rest of their working lives.

In this situation management must find alternative ways to engage the commitment of the workforce. The route to empowerment described in this book is a tried and tested approach to constructively involve employees.

Conclusion

In order to meet these challenges top management needs to enter into a new kind of relationship with its employees. It is a kind of synergistic partnership, where each depends on the other for success. Employees will become more independent, more self-sufficent, more empowered. As we have explained, the pathway to empowerment is difficult and painful at times, but, for most organizations, it is the only way to go to achieve survival and success.

Progress checklist

Have you carefully considered the part empowerment will play in securing the success of your organization? ❑

Have you thought through how you will initiate action? ❑

Have you devised a personal timetable for action? ❑

When will you share your aspirations with trusted colleages and gather support? ❑

Appendix

A BEGINNER'S GUIDE TO EMPOWERMENT

How to get started

This note has been given to you because your employer hopes to involve employees more closely in the way your organization is run. The word used for this is 'empowerment', because the effect of the change is to give you and your fellow employees more power. You can expect to have more say in the way you work and how you relate to other people in the organization. If this approach is to succeed, everyone must learn to operate in an open, honest and fair way, starting with the management. People must learn to trust one another.

Every individual in the organization counts. Employees can be more than 'a pair of hands'. Directors and managers want to listen to your point of view. Wherever possible, managers will let you and the people who work with you make more of the day-to-day decisions, but some decisions will still have to be made by management. Again, wherever possible they will seek your views and try to take these into account before any final decisions are made.

You and the people who work with you will be encouraged to work as a team and cooperate closely with all the people in other sections you deal with day by day. You will be asked to regard yourself as a member of an organization-wide team that is seeking the success of the organization. From time to time you will work closely with people from other departments. When you do, you will be regarded as a full member of the team. Your point of view will matter and you will be expected to listen to what other people have to say as well.

The management and your colleagues at work will recognize that you have your own priorities outside work – especially your family. These priorities and demands on you must be in balance if you are to give of your best at work and outside it. Management will recognize this and not make demands on you that will put you under undue stress. At work, you will be able to develop further team-working skills – how to listen to people, criticize constructively and work with others to achieve success.

Within the work context, management will still have the responsibility to set goals, provide premises, machinery and equipment and working materials. However, you will have the right to question their decisions and have their reasons for them explained. Managers will have a responsibility to keep you and your fellow workers informed. They will tell you what is happening in the company. They will respond to your requests for information and report back on any suggestions you have made.

You will be expected to behave in a responsible manner, ask sensible questions and make helpful suggestions. You will be asked to act in the best interest of the organization – not the interest of yourself alone or of your section or department. You will be expected to attend to the priorities of the business as a whole. You will be expected to be prepared to accept training and development to help you to become a more competent and flexible worker. If you know a task needs to be done, you will be expected to do it – provided you can. You will *not* be expected to do any job for which you have not been trained and you will not be expected to put yourself in danger.

Does all this sound too good to be true? That depends on whether or not you think your senior management group is sincere about wanting to run the business in this way. What if you cannot believe that your management will sustain efforts at empowerment? You must be careful. Test them out. Give them time. They might surprise you. If, over a period of time, managers do not behave in a consistently open, honest and trusting manner, sadly empowerment does not stand a chance of success.

If you believe that management might be sincere and that the empowerment style looks like a very real possibility, what can you do?

- Attend any meetings called by management or by your trade union.
- Look for signs of openness, honesty and trust – if there has not been much openness and honesty in the past, give it time.
- Talk it over with your fellow workers.
- If you are a member of a trade union, discuss this with your representatives. If the union is supportive, well and good. If not, ask the trade union representatives why. They may have genuine reasons for withholding support. Work with others to resolve the problem.
- Accept sensible training opportunities offered to you.
- Look for opportunities to contribute your own ideas.
- Expect management to live up to their promises.
- Constructively draw attention to any management failures to be open and honest.

- A manager may revert to bullying or prevaricating when under pressure. One lapse can be forgiven, but if this behaviour persists, first draw this to his attention, with the support of fellow workers. If this fails, report him to senior management.

- Do not expect miracles.

- Give the management your trust when they have earned it by their own consistent, honest and open behaviour over a period of time.

Management will trust you more with decisions and information as they become convinced that you can do your job well and you care about the organization's success. Managers want you to make constructive suggestions and be keen to find ways to make things work better. In an empowered organization, people are always on the look-out for ways of doing things better – providing a better service, a better product, a better delivery performance. People are keen to do a good job, and to help other people to do a good job, too.

Why should you cooperate anyway? The evidence is that, in organizations that seek to practise empowerment, employees are happier and healthier. They have a say in the way they work, more control over their lives, more satisfaction from work. Work can become a pleasant experience when everybody is on the same side. Other things being equal, an empowered organization is likely to be more successful, giving its employees greater job security and better rewards in the longer term. (There may be no short-term pay-off in terms of higher pay.)

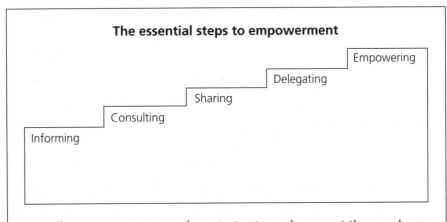

The essential steps to empowerment

Empowering

Delegating

Sharing

Consulting

Informing

At each step, managers must learn to trust people, respect them and earn their trust. As trust develops, each employee needs to acquire more knowledge and skills, accept increasing responsibility and be committed to the success of the organization.

Of course, empowerment cannot overcome some problems. If the bottom falls out of the market for the goods and services your organization provides, empowerment offers no slick solution. Even here, though, there may be a modest consolation. People who are used to working in an empowered organization generally fare better in the employment market. It might help you to get another job. The skills and insights you acquire may be helpful in other aspects of your life as well.

If you think you and your managers stand a real chance of success, give it a go!

Further reading

This list is provided for the senior executive who wishes to dig more deeply into some of the ideas presented or to read published accounts of activities used as the basis of some of the Snapshots. Although the books and articles are listed against particular chapters, they often contain material that is of general interest.

Chapter 1   What is empowerment?

Foy, N. (1994) *Empowering People at Work*, Gower, ISBN 0 56607 436 2.
A readable account of empowerment, focusing on managing change. It deals realistically with problems of delayering and downsizing.

Kinlaw, D. C. (1995) *The Practice of Empowerment*, Gower, ISBN 0550 60 75 709.
Covers the essential ways of helping organizations to make the most of their people's intelligence and skills.

Chapter 2   Benefits and pitfalls

Andrews, J., 'Lucrative Involvement', *Personnel Today*, 12 October 1993, page 39.
Reports six case studies demonstrating improvements in profitability that have occurred as a result of employee involvement.

Black, O. and Cartledge, S. (1996) *Empowerment: Any life left?*, Smythe Dorward Lambert – the Centre for Communication Development.
This report explores the benefits and boundaries of empowerment and how companies can use it profitably.

Crouch, N., 'Winning Ways', *People Management*, 25 September 1997, page 40.
A survey of successful strategies in commercial and public-sector organizations. It concluded that empowerment is an essential ingredient – although the word itself was disliked.

Chapter 3   Managing the culture change

Baron. A., 'Winning Ways with Culture', *Personnel Management*, October 1994, page 64.
Analyzes the results of a survey of 15 organizations grappling with the management of change.

Marchington, M. (1992) *Managing the Team: A guide to successful employee involvement*, Blackwell, ISBN 0 631 18677 8.
Describes employee involvement methods and includes a framework to aid in the selection of methods.

Ridgeway, C., and Wallace, B. (1995) *Empowering Change: The role of people management*, Institute of Personnel and Development, ISBN 0 85292 627 8.
Explores the role of human resource personnel in supporting the management of change.

Wilkinson, T. (1989) *All Change at Work: The human dimension*, Institute of Personnel and Development, ISBN 0 85292 414 3.
Describes 16 case studies where change has been successfully implemented.

Chapter 4   Rewards and empowerment

Armstrong, M. (1996) *Employee Reward,* Institute of Personnel and Development, ISBN 0 85292 623 5.
A thorough review of rewards and their relationship to motivation.

Ashton, C. (1994), *BICC's Blackley People Programme*, Vol. 7, No. 5, page 10.

Bott, K., 'Reinforcing and Developing Teamwork in Manufacturing', *TIM News*, June 1994 issue of the bulletin of the Tavistock Institute network.

Bott, K., and Hill, J., 'Change Agents Lead the Way', *Personnel Management*, August 1994, page 24.
These three articles flesh out the organizational changes at BICC Blackley, in particular the move to single status and the new reward system.

Chapter 5   Choosing the approach

Collard, R. (1993) *Total Quality: Success through people*, Institute of Personnel Management, ISBN 0 8592 511 5.
Describes how to achieve quality management by using appropriate systems and involving people.

Develin and Partners (1989) *Report on the Effectiveness of Quality Improvement Programmes in British Industry*, Develin and Partners.
Clearly demonstrates the need to engage the workforce and to commit adequate resources to quality improvement programmes to avoid failure.

Oakland, J. S. (1989) *Total Quality Management*, Butterworth-Heinemann, ISBN 0 7506 0084 5.
Explains, with practical examples, the basic concepts of TQM and how to introduce these practices, taking fully into account the people dimension.

Pricket, R., 'Alive and Kicking', *People Management*, 15 May 1997, page 28.
Organizational changes at The Natural History Museum.

Wellins, R., and Rick, S., 'Taking Account of the Human Factor', *People Management*, 19 October 1995, page 30.
This article explains clearly why business process re-engineering initiatives fail when the people dimension is not taken seriously.

Chapter 6   Initiating change

Belbin, R. M. (1981) *Management Teams: Why they succeed or fail*, Heinemann, ISBN 343 90127 X (a revised version is available).
This definitive work on management teams shows how the personal characteristics can be taken into account in choosing and supporting winning teams.

Guest, D., *et al.* (1996) *The State of the Psychological Contract in Employment*, (Issues in People Management, No. 16), Institute of Personnel and Development, ISBN 0 85292 688 X.
This telephone-based research explores the way people view the employment contract.

Singer, E. J. (1974) *Effective Management Coaching*, Institute of Personnel Management, ISBN 0 85292 248 5.
A thorough account of the art and practice of coaching that has not been bettered.

Stewart, A. M. (1994) *Empowering People*, Pitman, ISBN 0 27360 344 2.
Offers a step-by-step guide for managers to the techniques used in empowerment.

Chapter 7   Working relationships

Industrial Society (1995) *Employee Consultation: Managing best practice*, Industrial Society.
Booklet based on a survey. Explores best practice in setting up and managing employee consultation.

Marchington, M., *et al.* (1992) *New Developments in Employee Involvement*, University of Manchester Institute of Science and Technology.
This research study focuses on current practices in introducing and maintaining involvement.

Wheatley, R., and Parker, N. (1995) *Empowerment: Self-directed work teams*, Institute of Management Foundation, ISBN 0 85946 257 9.
Presents an overview of the theory and practice of empowerment and self-directed work teams, together with case studies and sources of training aids.

Chapter 8   Informing people

Blakstad, M., and Cooper, A. (1995) *The Communicating Organization*, Institute of Personnel and Development, ISBN 0 85292 575 1.
Communications within organizations is discussed, illustrated by case studies, including Price Waterhouse, Meridian Broadcasting and Nuclear Electric.

Wilkinson, T. (1989) *The Communications Challenge: Personnel and PR perspectives*, Institute of Personnel and Development, ISBN 0 08292 413 5.
Provides a comprehensive review of methods of communications within organizations.

Chapter 9   Generating feedback

Industrial Society (1995) *Upward Communications: Managing best practice*, Industrial Society.

Booklet based on a survey. Explores best practice in setting up and managing feedback from employees.

Johnson, R., and Williams, T., 'Cadbury Teams get Cracking on an Egg', *Transition*, June 1988, page 11.

An account of the introduction of teamwork at the Creme Egg Plant at Cadbury Limited, Bournville.

Chapter 10   Sharing and negotiating

Curzon, C. (Editor, 1986) *Flexible Patterns of Work*, Institute of Personnel and Development, ISBN 0 85292 376 7.

Describes the relationships between rewards and methods of engaging people to work. Includes subcontracting, temporary and part-time workers.

Hyman, J., and Mason, B. (1995) *Managing Employee Involvement and Participation*, Sage Publications, ISBN 0 80398 727 7.

The authors distinguish between participation and involvement and present a comprehensive review of the UK scene.

Johnson, R. (1984) *How to Manage People*, Business Books Limited, ISBN 0 09 172251 9.

Chapter 5 provides a simple introduction to the elements of negotiation.

Tse, K. K. (1984) *Marks and Spencer: Anatomy of Britain's most efficiently managed company*, Pergamon Press, ISBN 0 0108030 212 2.

Describes the company, including the management of people and trading relationships with other organizations.

Chapter 11   Managing business relationships

Syrett, M., and Lammiman, J., 'Developing the Peripheral Worker', *Personnel Management*, July 1994, page 28.

It is easy for employers to neglect the development of people who are engaged in flexible work patterns. Learning organizations need to include these people in their empowerment and development plans.

Chapter 12   Learning and development

Johnson, R. (1986) *Building Success Through People*, Business Books Limited, ISBN 0 09 160760 4.

A simple account of how the manager of a small organization or operating unit can determine what his people need to learn to succeed, and how to organize appropriate learning activities with minimal dependence on formal education and training.

Mumford, A. (1995) *Effective Learning*, Institute of Personnel and Development, ISBN 0 85292 617 0.

Provides insights into how people learn and how they can become more effective learners.

Reid, M., and Barrington, H. (1997) *Training Interventions*, Institute of Personnel and Development, ISBN 0 85292 660 X.

A comprehensive review of training and development, including self-managed leaning, competence-based assessment, benchmarking and learning organizations.

Chapter 13   Planned learning

Bramham, J. (1994) *Human Resource Planning*, Institute of Personnel and Development, ISBN 0 85292 554 9.
Provides a practical guide to planning human resources in organizations, taking into account empowerment values.

Johnson, R. (1990, revised 1997) *The 24-hour Business Plan*, Century Business Books, ISBN 0 7126 7779 8.
Explains how to draw up a business plan from scratch and identify the skills people need to make the plan and make it work.

Chapter 14   Empowering individuals

Belbin, R. M. (1997) *Changing the Way We Work*, Butterworth-Heinemann, ISBN 0 7506 2874 X.
Describes a new way to analyze the work that people do as a springboard for developing flatter organizations that aspire to excellence beyond competence.

Chapter 15   Organizational learning and teamwork

Burgoyne, J., 'Feeding minds to grow the business', *People Management*, 21 September, 1995, page 22.
Explores the concepts that underpin the learning organization.

Johnson, R. (1995) *Perfect Teamwork*, Arrow Business Books, ISBN 0 09 950541 X.
Describes practical steps to take to achieve teamwork in an organization.

Johnson, R. (1995), 'Towards the Learning Organization', *The Human Resource Management Yearbook*, AP Information Services, ISBN 0 906247 57 8.
Describes the characteristics of a learning organization and steps to take to achieve the necessary transformation in culture.

Senge, P. M. (1990) *The Fifth Discipline*, Century Business Books, ISBN 0 7126 5687 1.
A seminal and thoughtful account of how to build a learning organization.

Chapter 16   Leading an empowered organization

Grundy, T. (1993) *Implementing Strategic Change*, Kogan Page, ISBN 0 7494 0745 X.
A practical guide to the change process with an emphasis on the kind of leadership required. Case studies of change within Dowty, Prudential and ICL included.

Ridgeway, C., and Wallace, R. (1996) *Leadership for Strategic Change*, Institute of Personnel and Development, ISBN 0 85292 613 8.
Focuses on the leadership qualities required by people who seek to lead major change programmes.

Chapter 17   Facing the future

Axel, H. (1997) 'Implementing the New Employment Contract', *HR Executive Review*, Vol 4, No. 4, ISSN 1060-930X.

Report of a comprehensive survey on the future of employee relations, covering 92 major international organizations.

Binney, G., and Williams, C. (1997) *Leaning into the Future*, Nicholas Brealey Publishing, ISBN 1 85788 083 8.

A stimulating exposition of an approach that combines leading and learning in the management of change. It advocates a leadership style that provides clear direction, but also listens to people and allows space for individual initiative.

Index

Bold type is used to indicate where topics are defined or explored in depth.

360 degree assessment, 51, 160
ability, 42, 63–64, 107, 171–181, 178
achievement, 55
appraisals, 51, **159–160**
attitude surveys, 80
authority, 5, 23–24, **37**, 182–183

belonging, 54
benefits (from empowerment), **19–21**
blame, 8
bonus schemes, 52
brainstorming, 120–121
briefing groups, 104–105, 119–120
business plans, 63, 166
business process re-engineering, *see* re-engineering

change (initiating), 75
change (management, programmes), 22, 33, 40, 74
climate questionnaires, 81
coaching, 64, **88–89**, 128, **157**, 180, 200
command and control culture, 23, 36, **47–48**, 50, 127, 131, 159, 176, 197–198
command and control structure, 8, 93–94, 177–178
commitment (of employees), 5, 37, 175, 194, 199, 208
commitment (of managers), 23–24, **35–36**, 40–41, 115
communication, 21, **64–65**, **94–96**, 130, 199
community (concerns), 145–146
competence, 63, 169

competition (between teams), 49
concern questionnaires, 83
consultant, 79
consultation, 9–11, 37, 69, 78, **94–96**
continuous improvement, 9, 21
contractors (in-house), 144–145
core values, 206
counselling, **88–89**, **157–158**, 180, 200
criteria (hard and soft), **35–36**
cultural norms, 41
culture and rewards, 47
customer care, 20, 39, 59–62, 142–143
customer charters, 61

data gathering, 75–76
decisions, 5, 9–11, 13, 19–21, 24, 37–38, 127–136
degree of empowerment, 5–6, 9, 14
delegation, 13, **37**, 96, 97, **127–130**
developing ability, 42, 63–64, 107, 178
disadvantaged people, 35, 59, 181
discipline, 8, 24, 38, 66, 198–199
dynamic interaction, 123
dynamic learning, 156

education, 153–159
effort bargains, 132
employment patterns, 206
empowered culture, **47–48**, *see also* 198–200
empowerment matrix, 95
environment, 36
equal opportunities, 35, 181
evaluation (of learning), 170–171

expectations, 23, **24–26**, 82
expert-based studies, 76
extent of employee involvement, 5, 9, 14

flexibility (workforce), 21, 49, 66
focus groups, 59, **78**, 120–122
formal structures (for consultation),
   135–136
formation, **153–154**, 169

goals, 5, 34, 36, 192–193, 198–200
grievance, 38, 115, 199, 200

health and safety, 36
holistic view of organization, 187–189
honesty, 7, 9, 27, 88
house journals, 103
housekeeping (good), 21
housekeeping, 21

information management, **38–39**, 42
information, 5, 12–14, 68–70
interviews, 79
involvement, **9–14**

JIT, *see* Just in Time
job concepts, 59, **175**
joint decisions, 10, **130–132**
Just in Time (JIT), 34

knowledge, 154

large meetings, 41, 68–69, **115–117**
leadership qualities, 5, 200–201
learning (individual), 178–181
learning and development, 63–64
level of involvement, 5, 9, 14
levels (of involvement), 95

management code, 9
management style, 197–199, 207
meetings, 68–72

mentoring, **158–159**, 180–181, 200–201
merit-based rewards, 50
method selection, 68–70
monitoring learning, 170–171
motivation, 5–6, 36, 47–48, **54–56**, 170,
   191, 208
multi-directional information flow,
   109–110

negotiation, 9–10, **94–96**, **132–134**
non-financial rewards, 54–56

objectives, 33–35, 41
open learning, **168–169**
openness, 7, 9, 27, 88
opinion surveys, *see* surveys
opportunities, 33–34
opposition, 22
organizational renewal, 62

performance, 21, 47–48, 63
pitfalls, 22–27
planning, 15, 22, 66, 155, 165–168, 187,
   198
policy statement, 80
portfolio people, 144
power (and authority), **23–24**
prejudice, 35
problems, 33–34
productivity, 34
project, **40–43**, 80, 107–109, 180

quality management, 20, 59–62
quality, 34, 36, 53
questionnaires, 81–84

re-engineering, 34–35, 63
recognition, 55
redundancies, 22
relationships, 93, 118
renewal, 62
representatives (of workers), 14, 16, 33, 41,

50, 68, 105, 135
rewards, 7, 26, 38, 43, **47–56**

security, 54
sensitive information, 9
shared understanding, 193–194
shared vision, 192–193
shareholders, 141–142
shares, 52
shifts, 48, 108
single status, 49
skill-based rewards, 49
skills, 20, 24, 47, 66, 154–155, 167, 175,
    179, 201
span of control, 38
staff development, **38–39**
steps to empowerment, 9–10
strategic planning, 165–168
structure, 38, 41
subcontractors, 144–145
suggestion schemes, 122
suppliers, 145
surveys, 25–26, 59, 80, **85–88**, 122
systematic training and development, 64
systems, **36–38**, 42, 43, 93, 107, 188–191

talent (retaining), 206

team briefing, 104, 120
team member, role, 97
team processes, 190–192
teamwork questionnaires, 83
teamwork workshops, 67, **117–119**
teamwork, 20, **65–68**
teamwork, organization-wide, 190
total quality management, 61
trade unions, 14, 16, 41, 50, 69, 96, 135,
    207
training and development, 64
training, 153–159
trust, 7, 9, 23, **27–28**, 34, 88, 134

understanding, 155

validation, 170
values, **6–9**, 206
venues for workshops, 84
visits (exploratory), 79

winners and losers, 53
work groups, 93, 107–109
workshops (for management), 79, **81–85**
workshops (teamwork), 67, **117–119**
world trade, 207
written information, 101